The WORLD AT WAR
The CHURCH AT PEACE

A Biblical Perspective

by
Jon Bonk

D0067063

Kindred Press

Winnipeg, MB, Canada   Hillsboro, KS, U.S.A.

1988

THE WORLD AT WAR, THE CHURCH AT PEACE
A Biblical Perspective

Copyright © 1988 Evangelical Mennonite Conference
Box 1268, Steinbach, Manitoba, R0A 2A0

Published jointly by:
Chortitzer Mennonite Conference
Evangelical Mennonite Conference
Conference of Mennonites in Canada
Evangelical Mennonite Mission Conference
Canadian Conference of Mennonite Brethren Churches

Cover design by Ron Kroeker

Canadian Cataloguing in Publication Data

Bonk, Jon, 1945-

    The world at war — the church at peace

    Bibliography: p.
    ISBN 0-919797-87-3

    1. Peace — Religious aspects — Christianity. 2. War —
    Religious aspects — Christianity. 3. Pacifism —
    Religious aspects — Christianity. I. Title.

BT736.4.B66 1988   261.8'73   C88-098103-2

Published simultaneously by Kindred Press, Winnipeg, Manitoba, R2L 2E5 and Kindred Press, Hillsboro, Kansas, 67063.

Printed in Canada by Derksen Printers, Steinbach, Manitoba

ISBN: 0-919797-87-3

The WORLD AT WAR
The CHURCH AT PEACE

Table of Contents

Publishers' Foreword

Although every book is unique in some ways, this one is particularly so in several significant ways. For one thing, it arises from a "grassroots" pastoral response to the felt needs of a local church. In 1986 a minister of the Kleefeld (Manitoba) Evangelical Mennonite Church, Dr. Jon Bonk, felt the need for an adult elective Sunday School quarter which would strengthen the level of understanding of and commitment to biblical nonresistance in the congregation. In his desire to address this issue with a clear, biblically based, lay emphasis, Bonk felt the need to prepare fresh materials as weekly handouts.

As the quarter drew to a close, several members of the class felt somewhat like the lepers of II Kings 7 who felt the need to share with others the abundant provisions they had discovered in the abandoned Syrian camp. When the class members suggested that the EMC Board of Education and Publication consider making these materials available to other churches in the conference as well, the board agreed — with the further thought that individuals and churches in other conferences might also wish to share.

This led to the formation of our unique five-conference joint publication committee. A leaders' guide is also being prepared to assist those who would like further suggestions for group study. We now offer this material with the prayer that it may stimulate private and group study of this perennially relevant issue for the strengthening of God's people to the glory of God.

The Joint Publication Committee:
Al Hiebert, chairperson, Evangelical Mennonite Conference
Gilbert Brandt, Canadian Conference of Mennonite Brethren Churches
Henry Dueck, Evangelical Mennonite Mission Conference
Menno Hamm, EMC Board of Education & Publication
Bill Hildebrandt, Chortitzer Mennonite Conference
Stan Penner, EMC Board of Education & Publication
Rudy Regehr, Conference of Mennonites in Canada

Introduction

It is all too easy for us to believe in or practice something for no reason other than that it is our tradition to do so, and we are most comfortable with the familiar. Of course, there is nothing wrong with respecting and maintaining the views and behaviour patterns of our ancestors. Indeed, the touching story of the Recabites in Jeremiah 35 teaches us that faithfulness to the will and way of our forefathers is something which pleases God, provided it is not the sins of our fathers that we perpetuate. .

But as a people of God we are called upon to do more than unquestioningly uphold the beliefs of our ancestors. Each generation must examine the Scriptures carefully, thereby strengthening the noble traditions; clarifying, modifying and correcting the dubious ones. If contemporary Mennonite teaching on non-violence is seen as merely the residue of a quaint tradition arising from the shifting sand of a peculiar set of historical circumstances several hundred years ago, we can hardly be surprised if many among us question both its relevance and its validity in today's world. If, on the other hand, it can be demonstrated that for Christ's followers the Scriptures clearly advocate non-participation in lethal violence, we then have a foundation for our belief and practice that goes down to the bedrock of our sovereign God's will. Such a foundation will endure throughout time; and only those Christian beliefs and practices which are built upon that foundation are worth defending, maintaining and advocating.

Pacifism, for the purposes of this study, will mean simply refusal to participate knowingly in the taking of human life for any reason other than the direct command of God. While there is much that is worthwhile in the numerous expanded understandings of the term, it is my intention in the following chapters to explore only those questions pertaining to a Christian's participation in socially sanctioned and justified killing of other human beings. With an understanding of what it means to be a follower of the one who declared that his kingdom was not of this world (John 18:36), historical and biblical teaching on war will be surveyed, issues and problems challenging pacifism will be examined, and some practical implications will be suggested.

This book will argue that it is wrong for God's people today to destroy the life of another person. Death, the New Testament makes clear, is under Satan's jurisdiction, and will be the last enemy to be destroyed (I Corinthians 15:24-26). As such, it is not a means which in this age is ever appropriate for Christ's follower. Furthermore, we are saved by grace, not by good works. Every person alive deserves death, for the wages of sin is death. For any Christian to presume the right to take the life of another person is to suggest that some persons are more deserving of death than others, and that God's grace is not sufficient for some people. Finally, the Scriptures teach and human experience proves that there is none righteous, no not one. It is futile and dangerous to imagine that one's personal righteousness renders one fit to take the life of another less righteous person.

On the other hand, it would be wrong to overlook the fact that there have been and still are many devout Christians serving in the armies of scores of nations around the world. Most of these have not yet been called upon to take life in causes rationalized for them by their governments. Some of them are actively engaged in lethal violence right now. Without questioning the integrity of these brothers and sisters in the Lord, one must nevertheless wonder whether it is Christ who is leading them in such activity, or Satan who through them wields his most potent weapon, death. Although Jesus will one day return as the righteous judge of all who oppose his saving rule, it seems clear that in this age those who are his, understand that their mission in life is not to seek and destroy, but to seek and to save.

Ethan Hawley, the main character in John Steinbeck's *The Winter of our Discontent*, a powerful commentary on the American way of greed, rationalizes the erosion of his personal integrity by reducing life to the position that

> ... There are the eaters and the eaten. That's a good rule
> to start with. Are the eaters more immoral than the
> eaten? In the end all are eaten — all — gobbled up by
> the earth, even the fiercest and the most crafty (p.60).

In response to the considerable truth in this and similar points of view, Christians must, like their Saviour, number themselves among the eaten of this world. We are called to be givers, not getters; humble, not proud; persecuted, not persecutors; servants, not masters; proclaimers of the good news of peace with God through our Lord Jesus Christ, not dealers in death — the heavy weapon of the enemy of our souls.

Like any other important matter of faith and practice, so with the particular belief that is the subject of this book: it is one thing to give mental assent to it as a kind of abstract theological ideal; it is quite another to actually practise it in those circumstances where everything within you, except your faith, cries out for vengeance. As C.S. Lewis put it:

> You never know how much you really believe anything until its truth or falsehood becomes a matter of life and death to you. It is easy to say you believe a rope to be strong and sound as long as you are merely using it to cord a box. But suppose you had to hang by that rope over a precipice. Wouldn't you then first discover how much you really trusted it? (*A Grief Observed*, Faber, p.21).

No doubt many of us who, in times of peace and personal security, appear to be devoted pacifists, will discover only when our lives and the lives of our loved ones are at risk whether we really believe in this part of our Lord's teaching or not. Will we love our personal enemies and the enemies of our state when these enemies do all in their power to destroy or at best defeat us? Will we extend to these enemies the same grace that God in mercy shared with us? Time will tell. What is certain is that unless the Scriptures actually teach pacifism, it is not worth giving one's life for.

The short chapters comprising this book will, it is hoped, lead readers to biblically based personal convictions on the question of the Christian's role in lethal violence.

I make no claim to originality for the materials comprising these Sunday School lessons. For the most part, I am not a creator, but a collector. Much of what follows is simply a collage of the thoughts of others who have wrestled long and hard with both the theoretical and practical dimensions of Christian refusal to take human life. Their names and the titles of the books which they have written are at the end of each chapter. It has been a privilege to be able to prepare these lessons for the Evangelical Mennonite Conference (EMC). Members of the Adult Sunday School Class of the Kleefeld

EMC are to be thanked for patiently enduring the substance of these lessons a year ago. It is to them that this book is dedicated.

Jonathon J. Bonk
Kleefeld, 1987

Using This Book
as a Sunday School Guide

A Sunday School quarter typically runs for thirteen weeks. While this book contains only nine chapters, several of them warrant more than one week of discussion. It is suggested that two weeks be spent on each of chapters five, six, seven and eight.

Teachers will find it helpful to supplement this material with some of the excellent resources on the subject available free of charge from the Mennonite Central Committee Canada (MCCC) offices in Winnipeg. A catalogue of these materials is available upon request to: MCC Canada, 134 Plaza Drive, Winnipeg, Manitoba, R3T 5K9 (Phone 204-261-6381).

Chapter 1
The World at War

While it is unlikely that many of the readers of this book have personally experienced or participated in the ravages of war, news of war has become a staple in the daily smorgasbord of information served to us by the public media. That this should be so is hardly strange, given the fact that there have been at least 150 wars since the end of World War II, with an estimated combined death toll of over 16 million. Since 1960, there have been no fewer than 105 military coups, with military governments currently holding power in 56 nations (*Winnipeg Free Press*, May 25, 1987, p. 37). *The Carillon* further cites the following statistics:

> The year 1987 has been the best ever for manufacturers of military equipment and supplies.
> In total, $930 billion U.S. was spent, $1.8 million per minute.
> Of these amounts, too large for most of us to comprehend, the United States spent $293 billion and the USSR $260 billion. That represents 59 percent of world military spending; the rest was spent by the "developing" countries.
> Twenty-two wars were underway in 1987, a record high. The total death toll was estimated at 2.2 million — 64 percent were civilian casualties.
> On the positive side, U.S. President Ronald Reagan and Soviet leader Mikhail Gorbachev signed a treaty that will curtail certain military spending by four percent (*The Carillon*, January 13, 1988).

Tragically, while our planet is convulsed with the suffering of impoverished millions, governments of rich and poor nations alike spend astronomical sums on weapons of destruction, and many of our brightest scientists and engineers are devoting their genius to the creation of ever "better" (i.e., more terrible) and "bigger" (i.e., more indiscriminate) death technologies. It has been estimated that in 1986 global military spending ran at about $2 million US every minute (see World *Armament and Disarmament: Stockholm International Peace Institute Yearbook.* New York: Oxford University Press, 1986). In graphic terms, this means that at a rate of one dollar per second, it would take 32 thousand years to exhaust the amount spent for military purposes in 1986 alone! The cost of a single nuclear submarine far exceeds the combined annual education budgets of the world's fifteen poorest nations.

The writers of the New Testament frequently employ the language and metaphor of war when trying to convey certain truths fundamental to a correct understanding of the Christian life. In fact, one cannot read the Bible without coming to the conclusion that humankind is in the grip of a cosmic war which began with the rebellion of Satan against God, and which will continue until the return of our Saviour as Lord.

Every person is involved and therefore has a personal stake in this mortal struggle, although many may not realize it until they face the final enemy, death. There are no spectators in this war; there is no such thing as a neutral zone; there can never be a treaty, or a truce or even a cease-fire between the two sides.

Like all wars, so this one is filled with the horrors of hideous casualties, fatalities, destruction, carnage, treachery, and cowardice. But the stakes in this war are infinitely higher than are those of the conventional wars which are so much a part of our daily news diet. As John White points out in his book, *The Fight,*

> . . . War is not something that illustrates aspects of Christian living. Christian living is war. Indeed I would go further. Earthly warfare is not the real warfare. It is but a faint, ugly reflection of the real thing. It is into the real war that the Christian is to plunge. Wars on earth are but tremors felt from an earthquake light-years away. The Christian's war takes place at the epicenter of the earthquake. It is infinitely more deadly, while the issues that hang on it make earth's most momentous questions no more than village gossip (p. 216).

In war, not only is it a great advantage to know the strengths, weaknesses, tactics, terrain, and objectives of your own side; it is vital to have a thorough and accurate understanding of the enemy as well. We should be like Paul who, in II Corinthians 2:10-11 (in the context of a discussion of forgiveness) writes: "And what I have forgiven . . . I have forgiven in the sight of Christ for your sake, in order that Satan might not outwit us, for we are not unaware of his schemes."

If we are to be successful in the spiritual battle in which all of us are engulfed, we do well to study and understand the nature and extent of the forces which Satan brings to bear on the battlefield, and what our vulnerabilities and weaknesses are in the face of such an enemy.

Not surprisingly, the Bible has much to say about this battle between God and Satan, good and evil, righteousness and sin. And it spells out clearly the weaknesses and vulnerabilities which characterize us, and how we can take measures not merely to resist the devil, but even defeat him and his forces. Indeed the Bible would be entirely unnecessary were it not for the fact of this struggle.

We might accurately refer to the Bible as a manual of instructions for freedom fighters! We are, as long as we are in this world, insurgents, and we will be treated as such if captured by the enemy. We will be mercilessly destroyed by the enemy of our souls. But then this is the fate not only of those who are taken captive by the enemy, but of those on his side as well. For Satan's sole ability is to destroy. He can neither give nor sustain life of any kind.

A. The Enemy: Satan

Introduced in Genesis 3:1-15 as the serpent who tempted Eve to test the trustworthiness of God by tasting the forbidden fruit (see also II Corinthians 11:3), he is described in many different ways throughout the Bible, but is identified once again as ". . . the great dragon . . . that ancient serpent called the devil or Satan, who leads the whole world astray" in Revelation 12:9.

Satan is the archenemy of God. His sole purpose is to oppose God and destroy God's creation, including us. He and his vast and terrible forces, we are told in Revelation 12:7-17, waged war in heaven against Michael and his angels. As a result of losing the war, he and his hosts were hurled out of heaven to the earth, and here it is that he attempts to wreak havoc with all that is precious to God. ". . . woe to the earth and the sea," laments John, "because the devil has gone down to you! He is filled with fury, because he knows that his time is short" (Revelation 12:12). He is especially enraged at "those who obey God's commandments and hold to the testimony of Jesus" (Revelation 12:17).

4

Elsewhere, he is referred to as the god of this world, and as such, he has access to our hearts, deceives us, and receives our witting or unwitting obedience (e.g., Judas — John 13:2, 27; Luke 22:3; Peter — Luke 22:31; Ananias — Acts 5:3. See also Acts 26:18; II Corinthians 4:4; II Thessalonians 2:9).

As the "prince of this world" (John 12:31; 14:30; 16:11), he is ruler of a vast and powerful kingdom which stands in direct and implacable opposition to God, a kingdom populated by numberless subservient principalities, powers and demons (Matthew 12:24-26; Luke 11:18-19; Ephesians 6:12; Revelation 12:7-9). Paradoxically, his retreat began, and his ultimate defeat was ensured, with the death and resurrection of our Lord (John 12:30-33; 14:30; 16:11; Colossians 2:15; Hebrews 2:14; I John 3:8).

B. The Enemy's Objective and Bridgeheads

A bridgehead is "an advanced position seized in hostile territory, and defended as a foothold for invasion forces or for further advance."

It was through the sin of Adam and Eve that Satan was able to establish two bridgeheads in the life of every man and woman, boy and girl, born on earth. Biblical writers identify these bridgeheads as the world and the flesh. By means of these bridgeheads, Satan is able to carry out his destructive and deadly pillage of humankind to attain his objective, death.

1. The Enemy's Objective: Death

Every form of life on earth must die. By this means, Satan has access to every human being. Through death, Satan achieves his objectives. Jesus came, the author of Hebrews records, " . . . to destroy him who holds the power of death — that is, the devil" (2:14). Because death is so obviously an enemy, we need not say too much about it here, except to again point out that this is a bridgehead which will not be destroyed until Christ returns victoriously, having first ". . . destroyed all dominion, authority and power . . . [and has] put all enemies under his feet. The last enemy to be destroyed is death" (I Corinthians 15:24-26).

Although we loathe and fear death and fight against it with all our might, for those who have allied themselves with Christ, it has lost its "sting." In the words of Paul, "Death has been swallowed up in victory" (I Corinthians 15:54-55).

In the final volume of his *Narnia Chronicles*, C.S. Lewis depicts the final battle between the woefully inept and pathetically outnumbered forces of Aslan and the ruthlessly efficient and powerful Calormenes. As the motley collection of children and animals making up the forces of Aslan were inexorably, inevitably overwhelmed by the superior skills and numbers of their enemies, they were — one by one — forced to retreat or thrown bodily through the door of a burning stable . . . living sacrifices to the evil god Tashban. It seems, from the side of the stable overlooking the battlefield, that all has been lost, and evil is victorious.

But the view from the other side of the door is different! The weary battlers discover that the door leading to their doom is really the gate leading to the kingdom for which they have been yearning and struggling. They are home at last. The ultimate defeat which is death has been swallowed up in victory *(The Last Battle)*. Never let us delude ourselves, however; death remains the most feared and the most universally successful of Satan's intrusions into the life of every person.

Devastating though death might be, Satan has better-concealed and therefore more dangerous bridgeheads. Although these bridgeheads are just as universal as death, they are not as widely recognized or feared. Consequently, millions of Christians not only do not fight with all their might against them, but actually help Satan to maintain, employ, and even expand them in their own lives and in the lives of their families.

Satan, you see, is an infinitely complex and terrifyingly incomprehensible enemy who, when need be, "masquerades as an angel of light" and "his servants masquerade as servants of righteousness" (II Corinthians 11:14-15).

As such, he employs two bridgeheads of direct relevance to our study of the appropriateness of Christian participation in those earthly wars so much a part of human history:the world and the flesh.

2. The World

The Bible speaks of the world in three different ways: (a) planet earth: "The earth is the Lord's and everything in it, the world and all who live in it" (Psalm 24:1); (b) the world of mankind: "For God so loved the world that he gave his one and only Son, that whoever believes in him should not perish but have eternal life" (John 3:16); and, (c) the spirit of the age: "Do not love the world or anything in the world. If anyone loves the world, the love of the Father is not in him. For everything in the world — the cravings of sinful man, the lust of his eyes and the boasting of what he has and does — comes not from the Father but from the world" (I John 2:15-16).

It is the world in this third sense that constitutes a bridgehead into our lives for Satan and the forces of evil. This is the world of values, goals, aspirations, motivations, attitudes and preoccupations characteristic of every human society. We are born into this world, and it is bred into us so that we are scarcely aware of it. We can neither avoid it nor get rid of it. It will be there until we die.

It is the world of natural desire gone amok! "The cravings of sinful man" (in the King James Version [KJV] "the lust of the flesh"), "the lust of the eyes and the boasting of what we have and do" (in the KJV "the pride of life") are no more than natural human desires out of control.

To make of natural human desire for food, sex, comfort, possessions, natural security, or anything else, a principal goal or preoccupation is to welcome into your life the enemy of your soul, whose single purpose is to destroy you, and who is, in fact, capable of doing nothing more, nothing less, than that. Any desire for sleep, for recreation, for entertainment, for physical exercise, for comfort, for sex, for possessions, for money, for security, becomes a bridgehead for our mortal foe at that point where to satisfy it interferes in the smallest degree with serving and glorifying Christ (John White, *The Fight,* pp. 218-219).

3. The Flesh

The second bridgehead is what the Bible refers to as "the flesh." Paul uses the term with reference to the habits, instincts and tendencies of both the mind and the body left over from our fallen condition before we met Christ. He describes it in Romans 7:22-25:

> For in my inner being I delight in God's law; but I see another law at work in the members of my body, waging war against the law of my mind and making me a prisoner of the law of sin at work in my members. . . .

Peter speaks of "sinful desires" (in the KJV, "passion of the flesh") that "war against the soul" (I Peter 2:11). What is this bridgehead called "the flesh"? It is that within us which yearns to respond positively to the spirit of the age and to the wiles of the devil. It is fallen human nature dominated by, instead of being master of, human appetites. It is the seat and instrument of sin in us. It is the bridgehead which, if not constantly guarded, makes defeat of Satan and the world impossible.

C. Summary

In the context of this great conflict Christians must attempt to assess their participation in the lethal violence of earthly wars. All of creation is caught up in this great cosmic struggle. The enemy of all creation, including humankind, is Satan, whose sole objective is to destroy God's creation. Sin entered the human race through the fall of Eve and Adam, achieving for Satan the objective of death, and establishing two bridgeheads into every human life: the world and the flesh, both of which are especially dangerous. They are both so well camouflaged that they make us oblivious to their existence unless we pay special attention to our "Manual" which tells us how to recognize and deal with them.

No Christian would deny that the church has been specially commissioned by her Lord to accomplish tasks for which she alone has been properly equipped. Satan, the world, and the flesh sometimes combine to persuade members of the church that fulfilment of this mandate must, in times of national crises, be temporarily suspended or at least restricted. But do God's people ever have the right to barter their birthright for the mess of pottage which we call national security? Has our Lord indicated anywhere that God's followers should at certain times place a moratorium on their peculiarly Christian mission in this world and temporarily suspend active love for their enemies . . . provided that what is at stake is something as important as their nation's security or territorial ambitions? There can be no doubt that the weapons of the church's warfare are not carnal, but spiritual (II Corinthians 10:3-4). But are there situations in which it is expedient for God's people to employ contradictory carnal and spiritual weapons simultaneously? I do not believe so. Even when the contradiction between obedience to God and obedience to earthly authority is awkward and personally or nationally costly, Jesus must be Lord!

Satan, as ruler of this world, employs death as both a means and an objective. It is his primary weapon. Indeed, it is all he has to offer. Furthermore, in his guise as an angel of light, working through his subjects who often appear as servants of righteousness (II Corinthians 11:14-15), he specializes in distorting our spiritual judgements by means of the world (the spirit of the age) and the flesh (that within us which yearns to embrace the world's point of view), making Christians imagine that lethal violence is the way to accomplish the righteousness of God.

Let us not be unaware of Satan's schemes! The church's mandate is not a carnal but a spiritual one. Those called to follow Jesus are challenged to give up otherwise quite legitimate pursuits and natural loyalties (Luke 9:57-62). There is a deeper level of reality of which the world is deliberately oblivious, the world of "spiritual forces of evil in heavenly places" (Ephesians 6:12). Only those who have put their trust in Christ are equipped to wage war successfully and survive at this level. Earthly wars are simply symptoms of the great war being waged in this dimension, visible only to those who by faith follow Jesus. We dare not expend our lives and bend our energies to taking the lives of those whose violence is merely a symptom of this war. To do so is to neglect our calling for several reasons.

In the first place, for the Christian to engage the powers of darkness by participating in the destruction of life is little better than attempting to cure cancer by killing the patient. Such a "cure" is worse than nothing, and simply accelerates the inevitable.

In the second place, Christians who participate in lethal violence because they are told to do so by their government, do more than seriously undermine their ability to follow the Christ who loves and gave his own life for this enemy. In the eternal scheme of things, whatever human weapon we might employ against evil is no more effective than if we attempt to sink a battleship by pelting it with paper wads propelled by means of a rubber band. The line between good and evil does not lie between political ideologies, or nations, or classes, or religions or races; the line between good and evil runs through the heart of every man and woman ever born.

As an eleven-year-old boy living with my missionary mother and father in the politically turbulent border region of Ethiopia and Somalia, I recall two incidents which illustrate what I am trying to say. The first involved an unequal conflict between Ethiopian troops and Somali civilians. Political and religious hostility, which had been simmering for months, came to a head when frustrated Somalis demolished the Ethiopian police station by slinging heavy stones through its tin roof and mud walls. From their strategically located barracks on the hill in the centre of this frontier town, battle-ready Ethiopian troops marched down to the bridge in front of our house. They took up stations overlooking the river valley where Muslim Somalis were preparing for their evening prayers, and opened fire with rifles and machine guns. Although the Somalis fought back with stone-hurling slings, the conflict was short, one-sided, and bloody. In front of our eyes, seventy Somalis lost their lives, their weapons incongruously and tragically unequal to the conflict. Thus it is when Christians take up the weapons of the world to fight the battles of righteousness. Reliance upon such weapons leads only to the destruction of the people who use them.

In this same part of Ethiopia, my mother set up a makeshift clinic under a tree, where she would treat minor infections and diseases with her limited supply of medicines. It did not take very long before news of the potency of penicillin spread far and wide throughout the population. One or two injections of this mysterious fluid and the patient would be well on the way to recovery. All who came to the clinic wanted an injection of penicillin, whether they needed it or not! And they would watch, spellbound, as the white liquid was transferred from the vial to the syringe, and then from the syringe to the patient via the needle thrust into the exposed rump. What a marvel! So simple! So potent! Why had they not thought of this before?

It was two months after the first injection had been given when at first a trickle, then a torrent, of patients with huge abscesses on their buttocks began to show up at the clinic. A little investigation soon rewarded my mother's curiosity. An enterprising Somali, having observed the demand for penicillin at the mission clinic, had established a clinic nearby where he was able, by substituting "fresh" milk for penicillin, to offer injections at a fraction of the cost! Since the two substances looked the same and were injected into the body in similar fashion, he apparently reasoned that an injection of milk should accomplish the same miraculous cures.

Unfortunately, the two substances were only superficially similar. There was a level of reality not visible to this would-be physician, the world of germs and micro-organisms. Being unaware of this deeper, more significant reality, the Somali, by using unsterilized needles and syringes to inject raw milk into his patients, was seriously injuring rather than helping them.

Before we dismiss the dangerous and foolishly superficial view of medicine taken by this man, we should be aware that many people, including Christians, are no wiser when it comes to fighting spiritual war. Seeing the wars of this world at only the most superficial, surface level of reality, they set out to right wrong with wrong, thus compounding the injustice and underlying sin which gave rise to the war in the first place.

D. Questions for Discussion

1. Where do personal quarrels and fights originate, according to

10

James 4:1-10? What gives rise to the national and international quarrels and fights which we call war?

2. Can or should spiritual war be waged by means of the weapons of earthly warfare (II Corinthians 10:1-5)?

3. Is the righteousness of God ever accomplished by means of the wrath of people? If so, give examples, and explain James 1:20. If not, discuss some of the means whereby Christians can accomplish the righteousness of God.

4. Discuss the two illustrations in the summary section of this chapter. Discuss ways in which we sometimes fight our spiritual battles using inappropriate weapons? Give some examples of our tendency to see and deal with only the surface expressions of the cosmic war of which we are a part (see, for example, Matthew 16:23).

Chapter 2
In the World but Not of the World

Xenophobia is an English word which means hatred or fear of strangers. It comes from two Greek words: *xenos*, meaning stranger, and *phobia*, meaning irrational fear or dread of something.

In ancient times, and even among many contemporary peoples, a stranger is an enemy or, at the very least, a potential enemy — an outsider who doesn't belong, an unknown, a potential threat. Strangers in such societies are instinctively viewed with deep suspicion, frequently outlawed, driven away or killed.

In Canada we do not kill strangers, but we do view them as potential enemies, and our immigration laws are designed to prevent outsiders from gaining easy access to the privileges accorded to citizens. The visitor to Canada is welcome only conditionally, and only for a prescribed period of time. Then he must either leave or face deportation.

Suspicion of strangers reaches its peak when countries are in a state of war. Canada's treatment of some of its own citizens during the Second World War illustrates just how deeply engrained this suspicion of and instinctive hostility toward strangers is. At that time, Canadians whose ancestry happened to be Japanese, were deprived of their property and the normal rights of citizenship and were herded into prison camps. This shameful episode in our history, by no means settled yet, is a good example of the xenophobia which is part of the heritage we share with fallen humanity.

The Bible frequently refers to those who follow Christ as strangers on earth. Peter's first letter refers to Jesus' followers as "strangers in the world" (I Peter 1:1). In the world but not of the world, Christians in the Roman Empire were urged to live their lives "as strangers" (1:17). As "a chosen people, a holy nation, a people belonging to God," they were urged to live "as aliens and strangers in the world" (2:9, 11).

Marked by their loyalties, their behaviour, their values and their priorities as strangers in their own homelands, Christians have from the very beginning been the objects of that suspicion and latent hostility which are the natural lot of those who do not belong. Sometimes, when their presence is seen to constitute a threat to the well-being of a community, they have been persecuted, exiled or executed. While talk of persecution may have a strangely unreal and chimerical quality to those who live in Canada, Christians in other parts of the world often experience ruthless opposition as a matter of course. According to estimates appearing in the most recent "Annual Statistical Table on Global Missions," Christian martyrs in 1987 numbered over 300,000 (*International Bulletin of Missionary Research*, January 1987).

At no time is a Christian's foreignness more evident or less welcome than when he or she refuses the nation's demand to take the life of a national foe. Such a person is understandably branded a traitor and treated accordingly. Of course, not all Christians have scruples about killing in the context of war. Indeed, since the third century, most have regarded participation in war as an unfortunate but necessary part of combatting evil in a sinful world.

Christians in both camps profess to use the Bible as their source of authority in matters of faith and practice. The following pages will outline the nature of the problem, sketching representative ways in which Christians have dealt with the application of biblical teaching to the question of lethal violence. Then follow those principles which have governed the application of God's revelation to the issues of war in this book.

A. A Statement of the Problem: Some Givens

1. A Christian's conscience, conduct, and character are to be informed, regulated and shaped by the Scriptures. Thus, while every person is conditioned by and subject to the cultural, social, and civil structures of his or her time and place, the believer is held by God to be morally responsible and ultimately accountable to God.

2. War is not explicitly condemned in Scripture. Nor is it merely tolerated. Specific wars are commanded by God, who at times provides explicit instructions on how to conduct them (e.g., Numbers 31; Deuteronomy 2:24-3:11; 7:1-6; 20:1-20; Joshua; Judges. See chapter 6, "The Old Testament Sanction of War").

3. The New Testament stress on love for both friends and enemies is never directly applied to war. Nor does the New Testament

provide special regulatory guidelines for soldiers (an exception being those fruits of repentance described by John the Baptist in Luke 3:14). On the other hand, considerable attention is given to the question of Christian slave/master relationships. Three possible conclusions can be drawn from this glaring absence of information on the subject: Christian participation in war is either (a) compatible with, (b) totally incompatible with, or (c) irrelevant to, Christian morality. None of the New Testament authors address themselves to governments or to government employees per se (See Willard Swartley, *Slavery, Sabbath, War and Women*, p. 195).

4. A study of the Old Testament by itself would make it not only possible but necessary to argue for war (Numbers 31; Deuteronomy 20:1-4; I Samuel 7:8-10; 13:9; 14:37; Judges 20:18), selective genocide (Joshua 6:16-17, 25; I Samuel 15:1-9), slavery (Exodus 21:2, 32; 22:3; Leviticus 25:39, 44-45; Numbers 31:26), strict Sabbath keeping (Genesis 2:3; Exodus 20:11; 31:17), animal sacrifice (Leviticus 1:1-17; 3:1-17; 4:1-35; Numbers 28-29), polygamy (Abraham, Jacob, David, Solomon, were all polygamists), and numerous other practices long frowned on by the Church! It would be quite permissible and even desirable, on the basis of the Psalms, to curse and revile your enemies and to seek horrible revenge on them (Psalm 69:22-28; 109; 137:8-9; 139:19-22. See C.S. Lewis, *Reflections on the Psalms*, pp. 20-33).

5. Although, in Christ's own words, ". . . until heaven and earth disappear, not the smallest letter, not the least stroke of a pen, will by any means disappear from the Law until everything is accomplished" (Matthew 5:18; cf. Luke 16:17), the New Testament seems almost to have been written by worshippers of a different god, for no case can be made for divine sanction of any of the Old Testament practices mentioned above. The successful resolution of this apparently fundamental contradiction between the Old and New Testaments is the acid test for any Christian wishing to "correctly handle the word of truth" (II Timothy 2:15).

6. Civil government is ordained by God. Even wicked, idolatrous government is preferable to anarchy, and Christians are to submit to the rule of whatever power is dominant in their nation or province or city or community, " . . . for there is no authority except that which God has established" (Romans 13:1). In instances where biblical and civil injunctions conflict, however, Christians are told to disobey the government. Obedience to secular authority must always give way to obedience to God (Acts 4:18-20; 5:27-32).

B. Personal Participation in Lethal Violence: Three Christian Responses

Christian positions on the question of active personal involvement in their country's wars tend to fit into one of three broad categories (See Norman Geisler, *Ethics: Alternatives and Issues,* Ch. 9).

1. Activism. This is the view which believes that it is always right to participate in the wars of one's own nation. It is exemplified in American naval officer Stephen Decatur's famous toast, given at Norfolk in 1816: "Our country! In her intercourse with foreign nations may she always be in the right — but our country, right or wrong." John Crittenden, of American Civil War fame, likewise manifested this point of view in his statement on the legitimacy of the Mexican War (1846-1848). "I hope to find my country in the right," he said. "However, I will stand by her, right or wrong."

Few Christians would admit to holding this view. But in practice, this tends to be the position of most, due to the difficulty in distinguishing between a just war and a merely justified one. An individual's assessment of the moral legitimacy of his or her nation's war is necessarily based upon information which is strictly controlled by his or her own government. No nation has ever fought a war which its government did not justify. There are no exceptions to this fact. The rulers of Nazi Germany, for example, were able to rationalize their aggression convincingly enough to mobilize an entire nation of respectable, nominally Christian citizens to participate in a war which has seldom, if ever, been equalled for inhumane brutality or lack of legitimate justification.

It is hardly surprising, therefore, that Christians who in theory hold to the conviction that only some of their country's wars are just, in actual practice end up supporting all of their nation's wars, since all of them are justified.

2. Just War Theory. Most Christians, in theory, hold to one or another variation of the view that it is right and necessary to participate in their nation's just wars. In this category would be included: (a) wars of national defense against the unprovoked aggression of another nation; (b) preventative wars, in anticipation of pending attack (a position defended by theologian Harold O.J. Brown in the book *War: Four Christian Views,* edited by Robert G. Clouse); or (c) crusade wars, calculated to redress past atrocities of another nation. The sorts of practical problems faced by Christians who believe in any kind of selective pacifism are outlined in the section on "Activism" above.

3. Pacifism. Many and varied are the expressions of pacifism. Not all who advocate pacifism do so for primarily Christian reasons (see Robert Culver, *The Peacemongers: A Biblical Answer to Pacifism and Nuclear Disarmament*). John Yoder distinguishes between twenty-one distinct varieties of religious pacifism in his book *Nevertheless: The Varieties and Shortcomings of Religious Pacifism!* Whatever their differences, pacifists agree on this one point: in this age of grace it is never, under any circumstances, right for a Christian to knowingly take part in lethal violence.

C. Some Presuppositions

In their various statements of faith, most Mennonite conferences affirm a belief in the whole Bible as the inspired and infallible Word of God, as the supreme and final authority in all matters of faith and conduct. Accordingly, Mennonites understand the New Testament teaching on love to involve not going to war, not returning evil for evil, and avoiding selfish advantage over the next person. The way of love seeks the welfare of the other person, even if that person is an enemy, regardless of personal cost. (See the representative statements of several Mennonite conferences in the Appendix, p. 80).

Since the time of Constantine, most Christians have not recognized the inherent contradiction between Christ's teaching on love for enemies on the one hand, and Christian participation in attempts to exterminate the enemies of their nation on the other. This suggests that scriptural teaching on these matters can be interpreted variously, even contradictorily. Often, such diametrically opposed understandings and their concomitant practices within the church are a result of either (a) different ways of harmonizing the teachings of the Old and New Testaments, or (b) a hermeneutic that is subordinated to or conditioned by pragmatic nationalistic considerations rather than on objective, biblically sound principles of interpretation.

This being so, it is important before proceeding further with this study to set forth clearly, certain non-negotiable principles or "givens" which constitute the theological ribwork about which we will construct our understanding of scriptural teaching on the subject of Christian participation in lethal violence. As the devil himself demonstrated in Matthew 4, quotation of the Scriptures in defense of an opinion is no guarantee of its orthodoxy!

16

The following principles will govern our attempts to understand and apply biblical teaching relating to Christian participation in lethal violence:

1. The practice of love as set forth in the New Testament is not an option, but a moral obligation for all Christians in all times and in all circumstances (I John 4:7, 21; 3:23; John 13:34; Galatians 5:22; I Corinthians 13).

2. Christ's followers, and not human beings generally, hold themselves accountable to the values and practices of Scripture. Members of God's kingdom, Christians and Christian communities, are called upon to adopt and increasingly manifest biblical patterns of faith and life in sharp contrast to non-believers, whose lives are governed by the "spirit of the age." Christians are not called to conformity to the world, but to transformation into Christlikeness (Romans 12:1-2; Ephesians 4, 5; Philippians 2:1-11; 3:7-21; I Peter 1:13-2:3).

3. The missionary motif is central in Scripture, and lies at the heart of all biblical revelation. The church exists by and for the mission to which she has been appointed by God. A church without mission cannot survive any better than can a fire without burning. The mission of the church, which is Christ's body on earth, and of which Christ is the head, is to be and to do all that Christ came into the world to do and to be. All that the Bible has to say regarding the personal faith and practice of individual believers can be properly understood only if this great truth is kept paramount. And our Saviour, who so loved the people of this world that he gave his life for us, has commissioned his followers to complete his mission "to seek and to save" the lost, in contrast to nationalistic military mandates to "seek and destroy" the enemy. The two mandates are mutually contradictory. To obey one is to disobey the other.

4. The method of interpretation used by Christ's followers must enable them to listen carefully to the text within *its* context, and respond obediently and freely to the message of the text in *their* context.

5. On any given subject, care should be taken to avoid selective use of biblical evidence. The entire witness of Scripture, as awkward and obtuse as some of it might well be, must be considered. On the basis of selective use of texts, many bizarre beliefs and practices have been and continue to be justified:racism, genocide, adultery, human sacrifice and suicide, to mention a few.

6. No text must be isolated from its biblical context if the inter-

preter is to understand and apply it properly. Each text must be understood and used for its main, rather than incidental or peripheral, emphasis. This means that any particular biblical text must be considered in the context of the paragraph, the section, the entire book of which it is a part, and against the background of the social and historical context in which it was written.

7. Where specific counsel on particular topics (the "letter of the law") contradicts theological principles or general moral imperatives (the "spirit of the law"), priority must be given to the latter. This becomes necessary because we are far removed from the varied historical, cultural, and religious contexts in which the counsel was given. For example, although I Timothy 6:1-6 provides the church with specific directives on the topic of slavery, we should not conclude that Christians should own slaves so that they can be obedient to the counsel of this passage!

8. The modern interpreter should humbly acknowledge that the "world" or "spirit of the age" influences and may even hinder accurate understanding and application of scriptural teaching in his or her own life. We do indeed "see but a poor reflection" and "know in part" (I Corinthians 13:12). The lifelong challenge facing us as interpreters is to ensure that we do not evaluate God's teaching against the pattern of our particular world, but rather allow the Word to renew and transform our minds so that we can evaluate the world by God's "good, pleasing and perfect" standard (Romans 12:1-2).

9. Finally, a proper understanding of the relationship between the Old and New Testaments is vital to any correct application of biblical teaching to Christian belief and practice. How does a Christian resolve the dilemmas arising out of the striking differences which exist between the teachings of the two Testaments? Briefly, we believe that there is a time distinction between the Old and New Testament; one is to a large extent for "yesterday," while the other is for "today." These differences are such that one cannot assign to one period what belongs to another. Yet neither Testament can be properly understood without the other.

The obvious differences between many of the teachings of the two parts of the Christian Bible are not due to any essential change in God's moral will, but to the fact that God's creatures are bound by time and space, and can perceive morality only within these boundaries. When the Old Testament was written, the incarnation had not yet occurred; Christ had not yet died for the sins of the world; he had not risen victoriously over death; it was not possible at that time for "new creatures in Christ" to exist.

While the New Testament cannot be understood without the Old Testament, few would argue that Old Testament ethics and religious practices are normative for Christians today! The historical events described in the New Testament made, and make, a difference in the salvation, belief, and practices of the people of God. The people of God's old covenant and the people of God's new covenant are united, not in the particulars of their practices, but in faith which responds in obedience to God (Hebrews 10:19-12:13).

D. Questions for Discussion

1. What is the primary task of the church?

2. Is this task always a priority for the church, or are there occasions and circumstances in which God's people can, with God's blessing, temporarily ignore its unique mandate?

3. What kinds of activities or associations, if any, make it impossible for the Christian to effectively share the good news of forgiveness of sins and peace with God through the grace of our Lord Jesus Christ?

4. The Bible speaks of the church as "one body" with "many members" and Christ as the head. Can you envision situations in which the head might sanction the destruction of fellow members who might be on the other side in a war (for example, in situations where those in authority command it)?

5. How would you obey the distinctively Christian injunction to "love your enemy" in a time of war? What would be some likely consequences of obedience to God in such a situation? How would you cope with these consequences?

Chapter 3
War and the Early Church

A. Why Look at the Early Church?

The first three centuries of the church's existence, running from the Day of Pentecost described in Acts 2, until the reign of Constantine the Great (Roman Emperor A.D. 306-337), is frequently referred to by church historians as the age of persecution. Roland Bainton (Professor of Ecclesiastical History at Yale University from 1921 until 1962) calls this period the age of pacifism since there cannot be found a single Christian leader who, writing during these centuries, approved of Christian participation in war, even though there is evidence that there were some Christians in the army.

Robert M. Grant, the distinguished historian and author of *Augustus to Constantine: The Thrust of the Christian Movement into the Roman World* (New York: Harper & Row, 1970), says of early Christian attitudes to war:

> The only point, though it was a crucial one, at which Christian teaching sharply diverged from that of most Greek and Roman moralists was in relation to war and military service. Jesus' pronouncements about nonresistance left an indelible impression on the minds of the early Christians. Early Christian theologians condemned murder and cited war as prime instance. Manuals of church discipline refused to allow for the possibility of military service and insisted that upon conversion a soldier had to leave the army (p. 273).

There are two reasons why it is worthwhile for us to study the position of the early Christians on the question of participation in the lethal violence called war:

1. The early church was better able than later churches to correctly interpret the intentions of the writers of the New Testament, since culturally, historically, linguistically, politically, and socially, early church members lived in an essentially New Testament world.

Since we accept the judgement of these early church leaders who, between A.D. 70 and A.D. 170, determined the very materials which should be included in the Christian New Testament, would we not also take seriously their interpretation and application of New Testament teachings?

2. Contemporary Christian proponents of "just war" frequently refer to early church records for support of Christian participation in modern "just wars." For example, it is often pointed out that early Christians refused military service, not because they objected to war per se, but because of: (a) the idolatrous nature of military oaths and rituals; (b) a natural unwillingness to serve in the armed forces of a military regime committed to the extinction of Christianity; or (c) a naive, perhaps even heretical, view of eschatology, which regarded the return of Christ as so imminent as to render Christian participation in society unnecessary. Pacifists, on the other hand, hard-pressed to explain the presence of some Christians in the army, frequently do so on the ground that these Christian soldiers were engaged in police rather than military duties. Which view is most consistent with the evidence?

B. Evidence from Acts to Augustine, ca. A.D. 33 — A.D. 430
1. Absence of Evidence to A.D. 170

From the end of the New Testament period to the decade A.D. 170, there is no evidence whatever of Christians in the army. There are two possible reasons for this: either (a) participation was assumed; or, (b) abstention was taken for granted. The second explanation is the more probable for several reasons. In the first place, most converts to Christianity were civilians who lived in urban centres. Few were converted while in the army. In the second place, those who were converted outside the army had little reason to enlist, and many reasons against volunteering: they were not subject to conscription; as slaves or freedmen, many would have been ineligible in any case; and idolatry was a greater danger in the army than out of it. Furthermore, since the church throughout the second century refused to readmit to communion even penitent Christians guilty of apostasy, adultery, or bloodshed, is it not more reasonable to assume that the church withheld its members from military service rather than that Christians were permitted to serve without censure?

During this period, while there is no evidence of Christians serving in the military, there is also no specific prohibition of such service in the writings of Christian leaders. Nevertheless, there are a number of pronouncements of a general nature which have a bearing on the question. One such statement is found in the teachings of Justin Martyr (ca. A.D. 114-162), who wrote:

> We who were filled with war and mutual slaughter and every wickedness have each of us in all the world changed our weapons of war . . . swords into plows and spears into agricultural implements. . . . We who formerly murdered one another now not only do not make war upon our enemies, but that we may not lie or deceive our judges, we gladly die confessing Christ (Bainton, p. 72).

Justin Martyr suffered martyrdom at Rome under Marcus Aurelius sometime between A.D. 162 and A.D. 168.

2. Conflicting Evidence, A.D. 170 — A.D. 180

a. The Censure of Celsus

Celsus, a pagan philosopher and author of a scathing denunciation of Christians sometime during the last years of Marcus Aurelius (ca. A.D. 177-180), implies in his criticism that he knew of not a single Christian who would enter military service:

> If all men were to do the same as you, there would be nothing to prevent the king from being left in utter solitude and desertion and the forces of the empire would fall into the hands of the wildest and most lawless barbarians (Bainton, p. 68).

b. Condemnations of Military Service by Church Leaders

From approximately A.D. 180 until the time of Constantine, condemnations of Christian participation in military service appear with increasing regularity in the writings of church leaders. Although Celsus apparently believed that no Christian would serve in the military, he was mistaken. Christian participation in military service seems to have been more common in the eastern provinces and cities (e.g., Armenia, Syria, Palmyra) than in the western regions of the Roman Empire. It is well known, for example, that in A.D. 173 the famous "Thundering Legion" under Marcus Aurelius contained soldiers, recruited from the province of Melitene in southern Armenia. In the same region, early in the fourth century, an emperor who had attempted to enforce idolatry was defeated in battle by Christian soldiers! Syrian King Agbar IX, converted to

Christianity in A.D. 202, proceeded to make it the official religion of his province. It is doubtful whether such a ruler, on the eastern fringe of the Roman Empire, would have declared Christianity the national faith if, by so doing, he would have automatically deprived his nation of its army (Bainton, pp. 68-71).

Pacifism seems to have flourished within the interior of the Roman Empire, but not in the border provinces threatened by the barbarians. In any case, Christian participation in the military became common enough to elicit from church leaders strong condemnation of the practice:

i. Tertullian (ca. A.D. 150-240) makes frequent reference in his writings to the problem of Christian participation in military service. Throughout his writings he argued vigorously against Christian participation in military service. In his famous "Treatise on Idolatry" he wrote:

> But now the question is whether a believer can become a soldier and whether a soldier can be admitted into the faith, even if he is a member only of the rank and file who are not required to take part in sacrifices or capital punishments. There can be no compatibility between the divine and the human [military oath], the standard of Christ and the standard of the devil, the camp of light and the camp of darkness. One soul cannot serve two masters, God and Caesar. Moses, to be sure, carried a rod; Aaron wore a military belt; and John (the Baptist) is girt with leather (i.e., like a soldier); and, if you really want to play around with the subject, Joshua . . . led an army and the people waged war. But how will a Christian man go to war? Indeed how will he serve even in peacetime without a sword which the Lord has taken away? For even if soldiers came to John and received advice on how to act, and even if a centurion became a believer, the Lord, in subsequently disarming Peter, disarmed every soldier. No uniform is lawful among us if it is designated for an unlawful action (Helgeland, Daly, Burns, pp. 22-23).

This quotation sums up Tertullian's major objection to Christians serving in the army. In his view, military life and Christian life were mutually incompatible. One had to choose one or the other. It is only fair to point out, however, that Tertullian's demands upon fellow Christians were so stringent as to forbid employment in the civil service and in schools as well. No Christian, in his view, could participate in even the most innocuous of social conventions or earn his living in any occupation that might directly or indirectly contribute to the idolatry he saw all around him (See Henry Chadwick, *The Early Church*, pp. 91-92).

    ii. Origen of Alexandria (ca. A.D. 182-251), author of more than sixty theological books, was one of the most distinguished leaders of the early church. He is also probably the most thorough and articulate of the early apologists for pacifism. In eight carefully reasoned volumes, his answer to Celsus' charge was that by refusing to take part in military life, Christians were shirking their duty and putting the Empire at risk. Like Tertullian, Origen believed that the church was called and uniquely equipped to do battle with the spiritual forces of evil, and he argued that Christians, by their prayers and devout lives, waged war against evil elements which were at the root of all earthly violence, thereby, although unbeknownst to secular rulers, fulfilling their obligations as citizens. What follows is typical of his line of reasoning:

> Celsus urges us "to help the king with all our might, and to labor with him in the maintenance of justice, to fight for him, and if he require it, to fight under him, or lead an army with him." To this our answer is, that we do, when occasion requires, give help to kings, and that, so to say, a divine help, "putting on the whole armour of God" (Ephesians 6:11). And this we do in obedience to the injunction of the apostle, "I exhort, therefore, that first of all, supplications, prayers, intercessions, and giving of thanks, be made for all men; for kings, and for all that are in authority" (I Timothy 2:1-2); and the more one excels in piety, the more effective help does he render to kings, even more than is given by soldiers who go forth to fight and slay as many of the enemy as they can. . . . And as we by our prayers vanquish all demons who stir up war, and lead us to the violation of oaths, and disturb the peace, we in this way are much more helpful to the kings than those who go into the field to fight for them (Helgeland, Daly, Burns, pp. 40-41).

    iii. Clement of Alexandria (who died between A.D. 211-216) reflected a similar perspective in his writing, as the paragraph below illustrates:

> . . . in peace, not war, we are trained. War needs great preparation but peace and love, quiet sisters, require no arms nor extensive outlay (Bainton, p. 72).

Whereas, he argued, most people became emotionally inspired for war by martial music, Christians prepared themselves for spiritual war by means of the instrument of peace, the Word of God:

> If the loud trumpet summons soldiers to war, shall not Christ with a strain of peace to the ends of the earth gather up his soldiers of peace? A bloodless army he has assembled by blood and by the word, to give to them the Kingdom of Heaven. The trumpet of Christ is his gospel. He has sounded, we have heard. Let us then put on the armour of peace (Bainton, p. 72).

iv. Lactantius (writing ca. A.D. 304) is the last of the early Christian fathers to speak out clearly against Christian involvement in military service. His position is clear:

> God in prohibiting killing discountenances not only brigandage, which is contrary to human laws, but also that which men regard as legal. Participation in warfare therefore will not be legitimate to a just man whose military service is justice itself (Bainton, p.73).

c. Varieties of Early Christian Pacifism
While the early church shared a common emphasis on love and an aversion to taking human life for any reason, there was considerable variation in the particular expressions of that pacifism. Roland Bainton (pp. 81-83) sees the varied expressions of early Christian teaching on pacifism as fitting into one of three possible categories:

i. Legalistic, eschatological pacifism, such as that advocated by Tertullian, believed that a Christian's primary responsibility was to obey Christ. The social consequences of such obedience were the responsibility of God, who would mete out perfect justice at the last judgement.

ii. Gnostic pacifism, as exemplified by Marcion, combined an emphasis on love with an essentially Gnostic aversion to anything physical. The God of the Old Testament, together with God's wars, was rejected. The material world, with its parasites, plagues and wars, was intrinsically evil. Not only war, but marriage, was forbidden! This was hardly "Christian" pacifism!

iii. "Redemptive" pacifism, as expounded by Origen, regarded disagreement on means, rather than ends, to be at the root of tension between church and state on the question of lethal violence. Both church and state, it was pointed out, were interested in achieving justice and peace. But the means whereby these ends could or should be accomplished varied. The state, ordained by God because of sin, and run by sinners, was like a chain-gang of criminals engaged in useful work. The church, likewise ordained by God, was run by regenerated sinners, mandated and specially equipped to employ an infinitely superior way of bringing peace and justice to pass, the way of love. The self-giving love to which Christians were called and of which they alone were capable, was the most powerful means in the world for achieving victory over evil. Non-Christians, on the other hand, being incapable of this supernatural love, had no other course of action available to them, and must of necessity operate according to that inferior code of ethical behaviour involving coercion and bloodshed (Bainton, pp. 81-83).

d. The Collapse of Pacifism

The accession of Constantine the Great brought the pacifist period in church history to a close. It took twenty years of civil war (in which Christianity itself was an issue) before Constantine was able to defeat the other contestants for the throne and assert control over the empire. Not surprisingly, Christian hopes, prayers, and even arms, tended to gravitate toward Constantine, since he advocated toleration rather than persecution of Christians. And when, with the standard of the cross, Constantine defeated the enemies of the church, he was hailed as the Lord's Anointed.

In the popular mind, the fusion of Rome and Christianity over against barbarian and pagan had been gaining ground throughout the third and fourth centuries, thanks to the vicious persecution of Christians initiated by emperors originating from the half barbarian provinces in the region of the Danube: Maximinus Thrax, Decius, Diocletian, Galerius, and Maximinus Daza. With the victory of Constantine, the marriage between the Christian church and the Roman state rendered pacifism obsolete.

By the time of Theodosius II (early fifth century) the pacifism of earlier Christianity had become so radically transformed that soldiers polluted by pagan rites were excluded from the army, and only Christians could serve in the armed forces!

26

C. The Rationale for Early Christian Pacifism

While there are no credible scholars who argue that the early church did not actively discourage its members from serving in the military, several explanations as to why this should have been so, have been suggested by a study of the evidence:

1. Idolatry. Some argue that the primary reason for early Christian pacifism is to be found in the idolatry associated with military service of the time. The cult of emperor worship was prevalent. Officers were called upon to render appropriate sacrifice in prescribed ways on stipulated occasions. Participation by attendance was required of lowly privates. Idolatry was, thus, unavoidable.

2. Hostility to Rome. Others speculate that early Christians were pacifists, not for theological reasons, but simply because Rome was a persecuting power. Why should Christians fight for the maintenance of an empire which slaughtered them?

3. Eschatology. Still others argue that the early Christian antimilitarism was rooted in nothing more than a profound indifference to the affairs of this world. With the imminent return of the Lord, the earthly empire of Caesar would pass away, so there was no purpose to be gained and much to be lost by serving in Rome's armies.

4. The Way of Love. The most obvious reason for early Christian refusal to serve in the military is found in the pages of the New Testament and in the writings of early Christian leaders. Love of enemies was, in the words of Tertullian, the "principle precept." "If we are enjoined to love our enemies," he asked, "whom have we to hate? If injured we are forbidden to retaliate. Who then can suffer injury at our hands?" (Bainton, p. 77). The early church saw clearly the inherent incompatibility between Christian love for enemies, on the one hand, and Christian participation in that killing of enemies called war, on the other.

In later times, the attitude of love and the act of killing were harmonized on the rather dubious grounds that since destruction of the body did not entail the annihilation of the soul, and since the soul was more important than the body, the body could be tortured and killed with impunity, provided such action aided the soul in its journey to heaven. This was the rationale behind the inquisition of the Dark Ages and the Crusades.

While this chain of logic may seem somewhat farfetched, it is little different from that employed by contemporary "just-war" advocates, who imagine that justice and peace will result from killing the bodies of enemies. It is clear the earliest church had an aversion to participation in lethal violence, and therefore to military service in time of war. It is also clear that the chief objection to war lay in the belief that killing was wrong. Thus, those few early Christian writers who did sanction military service did so only on the condition that such service be restricted to police functions and entail no bloodshed.

In peacetime, in an empire where the army was vested with the functions of a police force, one could be a soldier all his life without killing anyone. In the city of Rome, for example, fire protection and the keeping of the peace were assigned to a military unit. Other services assigned to the military included care of public transport and the mails, supervision of public projects, and secretarial duties. Because of the diverse functions of Roman soldiers, there were Christian leaders who forbade only the taking of life, not military service as such (see Bainton, pp. 79-81).

D. Augustine's "Just War" Theory

Augustine, Bishop of Hippo (A.D. 354-430), lived at a time when Rome was threatened with an impending invasion of barbarians. Christianity had by his time been the official religion of the Empire for almost one hundred years. There was widespread fear, reminiscent of the North American fear of Communists, that if the Empire were overcome by the barbarians, the church and Christian values would also necessarily be destroyed. Ironically, less than four centuries after having miraculously thrived, despite every effort of a hostile state to annihilate it, the church was reduced to the pathetic notion that Christian values could not survive without government help!

Understanding that the "Christian" empire would defend itself against the barbarian invaders, and knowing that the behaviour of Christian armies should be different from that of barbarian armies, Augustine (A.D. 354-430) outlined the terms under which a Christian might wage war, on the apparent assumption that one side is completely in the right, and the other side completely in the wrong:

1. The war must be properly declared by a legitimate authority.

2. War must be used only as a last resort, after all other means have failed.

3. The intention of war must be to restore peace and bring about justice.

4. The war must be waged with moderation. The lives of ordinary citizens must be protected. The force used must be in keeping with

the objective.

As a matter of historical record, the barbarian threat was real: the barbarians invaded; the Christians fought; the Christians were defeated. According to the line of reasoning which had given rise to Augustine's "just war" theory, the church, and along with it Christian values, should have disappeared. But the fact is, the church was not destroyed; Christian values did not disappear. Instead, it was the barbarians who changed. Indeed, in time the evangelization of the world by Christian missionaries could be traced to this apparently cataclysmic defeat. In fighting, Christians accomplished less than nothing, sending to eternity barbarians who might otherwise have put their faith in Christ. The Body of Christ cannot be destroyed by the weapons of this world. The greatest peril lies not outside, but inside the church.

E. Questions for Discussion

Study the passages below to see whether or not you think a case can be made for Christian participation in war on the basis of these texts. If not, why not? If so, on what basis? Matthew 8:5-13; 10:34; 26:52; Mark 12:13-17; Luke 11:21-22; 22:36-38; John 2:14-16; 15:13; Romans 13:1-7.

F. For Further Reading

Bainton, Roland H. *Christian Attitudes toward War and Peace: A Historical Survey and Critical Re-Evaluation.* Nashville: Abingdon Press, 1960.

Helgeland, John, Robert J. Daly, and J. Patout Burns. *Christians and the Military: The Early Experience.* Philadelphia: Fortress Press, 1985.

Hornus, Jean-Michel. *It Is Not Lawful for Me to Fight: Early Christian Attitudes toward War, Violence, and the State* (Revised Edition). Scottdale: Herald Press, 1980.

Chapter 4
The New Testament's Apparent Sanction of Violence

Since the time of Constantine the Great (Roman Emperor Flavius Valerius Constantinus, A.D. 306-337), the church has tended not only to allow but even encourage Christian participation in certain' kinds of lethal violence. The theologies of those who find in the Bible divine sanction for taking of life by Christians tend to fall naturally into one of two broad categories: (a) traditional, and (b) revolutionary. We will outline below the salient features of each of these positions, and will see how their advocates justify their respective positions from Scripture.

A. *The Majority Position*
Christian participation in war is, for the majority of Christians, justified on the following basis:

1. God commanded to fight and kill.

> The God and Father of Abraham, Isaac, and Jacob, and of our Lord Jesus Christ, instructed his people of old to wage war when necessary and to slay the enemy. . . . These explicit instructions by God make it impossible to maintain that God prohibits the believer from engaging in war under any circumstances (George Knight, as quoted by Swartley, p. 97).

2. God honoured military leaders.

> If the waging of war and the military profession were in themselves wrong and displeasing to God, we should have to condemn Abraham, Moses, Joshua, David, and all the rest of the holy fathers, kings, and princes, who served God as soldiers and are highly praised in Scriptures because of this service (Arthur Holmes, as quoted by Swartley, p. 98).

3. Many New Testament passages appear to endorse war.

a. The teachings and actions of Jesus justify war:

i. He prophesied that there would be wars in the future: Matthew 24:1-8; Luke 19:41-44; 21:20-24.

ii. He recognized that faith in him would bring dissension: Matthew 10:34-36; Luke 12:49-53; 14:25-26.

iii. He recognized the virtue of being prepared: Luke 11:21-22; 14:31; 12:37-40; 22:35-36.

iv. He implied that war is justifiable under certain conditions: John 18:35-36; Mark 12:1-9; Matthew 18:6-7.

v. He commended the centurion, a man of war: Matthew 8:5-10, 13.

vi. He advocated obedience to authority: Mark 12:13-17.

vii. He advocated paying of taxes, knowing that they might be used by the Roman war machine: Mark 12:13-17.

viii. He demanded self-sacrifice, even to the point of death, in defence of values that are more important than life: Luke 9:23-25; Matthew 20:25-28; John 15:12-13.

ix. He portrayed God as One who would use force in awarding punishment:Matthew 18:23-25; 13:40-42; 24:29-31, 45-51; Luke 19:11-27; 10:10-15.

x. He drove the moneychangers from the temple: John 2:13-16.

b. John the Baptist did not ask soldiers to quit their service, but instructed them rather how to be good soldiers: Luke 3:14.

c. Peter was sent to Cornelius, the centurion, who is described as God-fearing, righteous, and acceptable to God:Acts 10.

d. The apostolic writings teach subjection to authority:Romans 13; I Peter 2:17ff.

e. God as warrior is basic to Jewish and Christian theology: Exodus 15:3-4; Psalm 24:8.

B. Theologies of Revolution and Liberation

Certain theologians today endorse violence as part of God's program to achieve liberation and justice for the oppressed. Pointing out that violence is an integral part of salvation history in the Bible, and that God always takes the side of the oppressed in the struggle to achieve liberation and justice, they argue that God's people, because they are in history, cannot avoid being a part of this struggle. They are involved in violence . . . either for the oppressed, or against the oppressed. Neutrality is not an option.

The following points are among those raised as evidence of biblical support for this position:

1. Exodus: Liberation from oppression is central to biblical thought.

The decisive event of Israel's history was the exodus from Egypt, whereby God freed an oppressed people by destroying those who enslaved them (Exodus 6:6; 15:1-2). Numerous Old Testament texts depict God acting for the oppressed against their oppressors (e.g., Isaiah 10:1-4; Micah 2:1-5; Zechariah 7:8-14).

2. Justice: God's justice requires destruction before building up (Jeremiah 1:10; Luke 1:50-53).

Biblical faith calls God's people to side with the oppressed in the revolutionary struggles of history. The Bible clearly advocates violence to achieve justice. For example, in the death penalty (Genesis 9:6; Exodus 17:4; 21:12-17), God not only permitted but commanded violent death as an act of justice. Jesus quoted Exodus 21:17 in Mark 7:9-11; therefore Jesus explicitly approves the use of violence in the pursuit of justice. Texts such as Luke 22:36; Matthew 10:34; Matthew 23; and John 2:14-22 show that Jesus never disapproved his Father's conduct to execute vindictive justice against evil and oppression. Thus, the violence of the capitalist or communist systems, resulting in the death of millions of human beings year after year by hunger, oppression and war, should be dealt with violently. Violent struggle against such injustice is not only permitted, but required of Christians. Numerous biblical texts correlate God's demand for justice with God's liberation of the people from oppression and with the threat of captivity if injustice continues (Amos 2: 6-16; 3:2; 4:2; 6:12; 8:4-8; 9:7-8; Hosea 12:6; 13:5-8; Micah 6:8).

3. Messianic hope: The messianic hope in the Bible is defined chiefly as liberation and justice (Isaiah 32:17; Psalm 85).

Although traditional and revolutionary theologies seem, on the surface, to have nothing in common, a closer look quickly reveals that both rely on a particular use of the Old Testament to provide biblical warrant for the particular violence which they may wish to advocate or justify. In the case of traditionalists, that lethal violence which is perpetuated by or on behalf of the state is legitimate; to the liberationist, on the other hand, since God is on the side of the oppressed, lethal violence against an unjust and oppressive state is the will of God for oppressed peoples and for Christians generally. Both theologies of violence have considerable problems with New

32

Testament teaching but neither sees any fundamental contradiction between its position and that of Jesus and the early church. Indeed, as seen above, both make use of certain New Testament passages thought to be supportive of their position.

C. An Examination of New Testament Texts Used to Justify Lethal Violence

1. John 2:13-17. The argument which uses this text to prove that Jesus sanctions violence runs something like this: In using the whip, Jesus used violence himself; in using violence himself, Jesus gave his sanction to violence; a just war, inspired by righteous wrath, is sanctioned by Jesus.

The most obvious oversight on the part of those using this text to support Christian participation in war is that war is not fought with whips. There is a difference not only in degree but in kind between whips and nuclear missiles. On the basis of this text, the Christian may well sanction certain kinds of violence (e.g., spanking rebellious young children) but never the lethal, indiscriminate violence of war.

Secondly, a close look at the text makes it unclear whether the whip was used on people, or on the sheep and oxen which were with them in the outer court of the temple. It is important to remember that in the temple the priests were in charge, and had their own police present to keep order. If Jesus had actually used the whip on temple patrons, it is safe to assume he would have been arrested. However, to drive out the large animals with a whip is perfectly understandable, and there was little the Jewish authorities could do, since by having animals in the outer court of the temple they were violating their own laws. Notice the text is careful to point out that Jesus didn't use his whip on the back of those selling doves; he simply told them to "Get these out of here!" (v.16). Jesus' words and actions had the support of the law.

The outer court of the temple was the only place where Gentiles were permitted to come and pray. By closing it off from Gentile use, the temple rulers effectively nationalized the temple, making it a place for Jews only. By his action, Jesus was insisting that the temple should be open to all. This is a far cry from approval of war! (See Lasserre, pp. 45-48; McSorley, pp. 33-34).

2. John the Baptist (**Luke 3:14**) did not condemn the soldiers who asked him what repentance would mean for them. Therefore, it is reasoned, John the Baptist must have recognized the legitimacy of military activity.

Jesus did not reproach the centurion of Capernaum whose servant he healed (Luke 7:1-10; Matthew 8:5-13). In fact, he commended him for his faith. This demonstrates, the argument goes, that Jesus sanctioned involvement in the military.

The lines of reasoning followed by those who use these texts as justification for Christian participation in lethal violence are similar, so they will be considered together.

In the first place, the arguments arise from silence. On the same basis, one could argue that since Jesus did not reproach Pilate for his presence in Palestine as chief representative of an occupying power, he must have sanctioned Roman occupation; since he sanctioned Roman occupation of Palestine, he must sanction all military occupations generally; since he sanctions all military occupations generally, he must condemn all defensive wars against foreign invasions. On the other hand, he did not reproach the Zealots for their patriotism and their violent hostility to the Roman occupiers; in fact, one of his disciples was a Zealot, and Jesus did not reproach him; therefore, Jesus must have sanctioned all patriotic, violent resistance to Roman occupation; so he must sanction all resistance movements. He did not rebuke Pilate for having massacred the Galileans in the middle of their sacrifices (Luke 13:1-3), so he sanctioned the most brutal measures of oppression. One can sanction almost anything by this means.

Secondly, these Scriptures are at best shorthand accounts of their conversations with the soldiers. We have no idea what else was said; and we do not know whether these men became Christians when the church was born. After all, it must be remembered that "the Holy Spirit had not yet come" (John 7:39), and spiritual regeneration was not yet possible. It is rash to try to speculate how soldiers who did become Christians resolved their personal problem, since the New Testament is silent on the matter (See Lasserre, pp. 53-58; McSorley, pp. 36-38).

3. **Matthew 26:51-54** proves that Jesus was no pacifist. He summoned his followers to armed defense. He commanded them to buy swords, thus not only sanctioning the bearing of arms by his disciples, but commanding it, thus implicitly approving their use.

This passage and its parallels (Luke 22: 35-38, 49-51; John 18:10-11) are interpreted in a number of ways:

a. Jesus ordered his disciples to buy swords so that the prophecy could be fulfilled, "And he was numbered with the transgressors (Luke 22:37). The Romans, like all armies of occupation, would not tolerate the bearing of arms by private citizens. In order to be "numbered among the transgressors," Jesus asked his disciples to have swords on hand so that when he was arrested, he could be legally considered a criminal, having been arrested among men who were armed and preparing for insurrection. In fact, he asked his disciples to play the part of criminals, so that it would afterwards be noted that Isaiah 53:12 applied to him, and that he was therefore the Messiah.

b. A second interpretation argues that when Jesus commanded his disciples to buy swords he was giving his approval to the bearing and the use of arms by his followers.

Several comments need to be made with respect to both of these interpretations. If one favours the first interpretation, it must be admitted that the swords were more for symbolic purposes than for mortal combat. That is why Jesus was content with only two swords to defend twelve men. From the context, it is clear that his disciples did not understand this, since Peter uses his sword to injure the servant of the High Priest. Jesus wastes no time in putting a stop to this kind of activity, and he heals the servant's injured ear (Luke 22:49-51).

If one favours the second interpretation, a number of questions need to be considered: First, did Jesus really think that his disciples would be able to buy twelve swords at that late hour . . . in view of the fact that possession of swords by private citizens was against the law and that, accordingly, swords were very difficult to obtain?

Second, if Jesus really wanted each of his disciples to get a sword, why did he say, "That is enough" when his disciples had shown him two swords (Luke 22:38)?

Third, when Peter at the critical moment effectively uses his sword, Jesus rebukes him and heals the servant's ear. Why should Jesus have asked his disciples to buy swords if he was then going to stop them from using them when they were most needed? Was it because at the last minute, seeing that the crowd was too large to deal with, he decided to give himself up? But in that case, why was he satisfied with just two swords in the first place? Or was he thinking of his disciples using the swords in the period after his arrest? If so, for what purpose? Self defence? Against whom? If against the authorities, that would be against all New Testament teaching on submission to proper civil authorities. Was he suggesting an armed insurrection? The same reasoning applies.

Were they to use the weapons to defend themselves against personal enemies who might attack them individually? This too is against all New Testament teaching on personal retribution. And in any case, why should anyone want to attack the disciples personally? They were neither wealthy nor powerful. They were apostles, and conceivably might suffer attack for that reason. But violence is never sanctioned within the framework of the church and its mission, even if one grants that individual Christians may kill within the framework of civil society.

These literal interpretations are not adequate, and in any case, can hardly stand as evidence that Christ urged Christians to active participation in lethal violence (See Lasserre, pp. 37-45; McSorley, pp. 34-35, 39-43; Swartley, p. 254).

c. A third interpretation suggests that Jesus was using the word "sword" in a figurative sense, encouraging them to get ready for what would be perhaps the most difficult spiritual battle they would ever fight. This would fit in well with Jesus' habit of using language full of imagery, and it would not be the first time his hearers made the mistake of taking literally what he intended figuratively (e.g., Mark 8:15-16; John 3:4, 6:42, 52). As Calvin put it,

> Here is another example of dull and most shameful ignorance on the part of the disciples, that after being warned and admonished so often to bear the cross, they nevertheless think they will have to fight with swords of steel. . . . They were so stupid they never thought of the spiritual enemy (as quoted by Lasserre, p. 43).

4. Jesus said in **Matthew 10:34**, "I did not come to bring peace, but a sword." According to this, Jesus' kingdom will be established by the sword so he must approve of participation in war by his followers.

Here, it must be obvious that we do not have Jesus' sanction of Christian involvement in war. He is using the word "sword" figuratively. Luke 12:51 employs the term "division" instead of "sword." The context suggests that Jesus refers here to the consequences of taking his words seriously. The path of discipleship separates us from those who do not follow the same path (See Lasserre, p. 43; McSorley, pp. 35-36; Swartley, p. 255).

5. In **John 15:13**, Jesus declares that the ultimate test of a person's love is the willingness to give up one's very life for a friend. Therefore it is not only right but noble for a soldier to die in battle

for the sake of his country and loved ones.

Notice that Jesus did not say, "The one who kills his enemies for the sake of his friend shows love." Soldiers are taught to stay alive and kill. Of course many soldiers die trying to kill on behalf of friends. We can hardly argue from this text that war is the supreme expression of the love to which Christians are called. In this passage Jesus is urging upon his disciples a life of self-sacrifice, modelled after his own. Jesus laid down his life for his friends (disciples). He challenges his disciples to give up their lives "as living sacrifices" to him (v.14) (See McSorley, pp. 38-39).

6. According to **Mark 12:13-17**, we should render to Caesar the things that are Caesar's, and to God the things that are God's. Those citing this text as proof that Christians may participate in war argue that in religious matters such as worship, prayer, personal morality, we should obey God, while in secular matters, such as war, we should obey the state.

Actually, the question which led to Jesus' reply was designed as a trap. If Jesus had answered, "Submit to Rome," he would have been accused of not being on the side of the oppressed; if he had answered, "Refuse to pay," he could have gone to prison for inciting the people against Rome.

Note that there is no reference here to war or even to paying taxes for war. Jesus simply replies that Rome should be given her pathetic little coins, and God should be given God's due. From his teaching elsewhere, it is clear that God's due has precedence over all else. "Seek first God's Kingdom and His righteousness . . . ." Not even food and clothing needs should take precedence over God.

The only claim the state can have on a follower of Jesus is when it goes along with what God asks of us. The state has no authority over us in opposition to God (Acts 4:19,20; 5:29). Even if one were to concede that this text supports the authority of the state, given the context it would mean that people whose land has been invaded and occupied by a foreign army must not defend themselves or take up weapons to drive out the invaders. This is hardly an acceptable interpretation which Christians, who advocate participation in "just war," would be prepared to accept (See Lasserre, pp. 86-94; McSorley, pp.43-45; Swartley, pp. 254-255).

7. **Romans 13:1-7 and I Peter 2:13-17** urge believers to obey those in authority, not only because they might be hurt if they did otherwise, but because all authority comes from God. In obeying them they obey God. So when the state requires Christ's followers

to fight a war, they must obey.

These texts will require careful consideration when, in a later lesson, the question of the relationship between the church and state is dealt with. For now, let it suffice to point out that in neither text do we find sanction for Christian participation in lethal violence; rather, these texts approve of police power and civil law. Neither Paul nor Peter even once refers to "war" in these texts. "Higher powers" refers to civil magistrates; "sword" is the symbol of civil authority. From these texts, it is clear that the civil authority has the right to police (See Lasserre, pp. 83-86, 102-110, 183-187; McSorley, pp. 45-52; Hershberger, p. 295).

D. Conclusion

Attempts to use these New Testament passages as a basis for Christian participation in war do not satisfy the requirements of sound interpretation as outlined in Chapter 2. It remains to come to a more biblically satisfactory understanding of the Christian's relationship to the state in light of Romans 13:1-7 and I Peter 2:13-17.

E. Questions for Discussion

The questions below need to be considered by those Christians who consider involvement in their nation's wars a justifiable necessity. Discuss each one carefully.

1. Is it always right, only sometimes right, or never right for a Christian to join in a war of resistance against an invading army?

2. If it is always right or sometimes right, is it right for a Christian to fight on after the alien invasion has succeeded?

3. If so, for how long, and on what grounds?

4. If not, why resist in the first place, since the loss of life, and the anger and the hate generated, would not have accomplished the original point of defence anyway?

5. Should a Christian fight in obedience to a "government in exile"?

6. At what point can a Christian determine that the defeated state is no longer "ordained of God," and the invading state is ordained of God, and that therefore he or she can go to war for what used to be "the other side"?

F. For Further Reading

Hershberger, Guy Franklin. *War, Peace, and Nonresistance.* Appendix 2, "Some Difficult Texts." Scottdale: Herald Press, 1969 (pp. 297-307).

38

Lasserre, Jean. *War and the Gospel.* London: James Clarke & Co., 1962 (pp. 36-58; 81-144).

McSorley, Richard. *New Testament Basis of Peacemaking.* Scottdale: Herald Press, 1985 (pp. 33-52).

Swartley, Willard M. *Slavery, Sabbath, War and Women: Case Studies in Biblical Interpretation.* Appendix 2, "Pacifist Answers to New Testament Problem Texts." Scottdale: Herald Press, 1983 (pp. 250-255).

Chapter 5
New Testament Teaching Against
Lethal Violence

In previous chapters, two questions have been explored: (a) What did members of the early church understand to be their permissible or preferable role in the state-advocated violence of their day? (b) How are we to understand those New Testament texts which seem to sanction violence, and which serve as the basis of contemporary Christian rationalization of their own participation in lethal violence? In this chapter, we come to a third and even more important question: What do Christ and the writers of the New Testament actually teach about Christian participation in the state-sanctioned taking of life called war?

A. *The Context of New Testament Teaching*

In considering that the teaching and practice of Jesus' thought have a bearing on the question of his followers' participation in killing, it is important to understand that Jesus neither lived nor taught in a political vacuum. He was born and raised among a people and in a part of the Roman Empire notorious for its fanatical, often bloody nationalism. From the time when Nebuchadnezzar's armies laid waste the city of Jerusalem in 586 B.C., until the final terrible destruction of the city by Emperor Hadrian in A.D. 135, Palestine's story is one long record of usually unsuccessful bloody revolt against ruthlessly cruel foreign domination and oppression.

The oppression reached its climax in December 167 B.C., when the Syrian, Antiochus Epiphanes, after eight years of senselessly capricious and scarcely believable cruelty toward the Jews of Palestine, sacrificed a sow on the great altar of burnt offering in the temple area.

This sacrilege led to the Maccabean Revolt in which, after almost three years of bloody conflict, the Jews won back their religious freedom, rededicating their desecrated temple in December 164 B.C. A feast commemorating this happy event was instituted, and has been kept annually to this day. This is the celebration alluded to in John 10:22 (The Feast of Dedication), today celebrated by Jews around the world as the festival of Hanukkah. The story of the Maccabean period is found in the two books of the Apocrypha entitled I and II Maccabees.

Palestine was to enjoy an eighty-year period of national freedom, until 63 B.C., when Roman General Pompey took possession of Jerusalem, abolished the Jewish kingship, and made Judea subject to Rome. In 37 B.C., a powerful but corrupt Idumean chieftain named Herod, captured Jerusalem, decreeing himself "Herod the Great" in 40 B.C. It was this Herod who, having heard of the birth of a "King of the Jews," gave orders that all male children in Bethlehem under the age of two should be killed (Matthew 2:16).

After his death, his kingdom was divided among three of his sons: Archelaus, who was given jurisdiction over the southern portion of Palestine, but whose tyrannical rule led to his banishment and replacement by a Roman governor, Pontius Pilate;Philip, who inherited the northern and northeastern parts of Palestine; and Herod Antipas (the Herod of the New Testament), who presided over those parts of the land in which Jesus spent most of his life on earth, Galilee and Perea. His domain was given to Herod Agrippa in A.D. 39, before whose son (Herod Agrippa II) Paul would plead his cause (Acts 25:13-26:32).

Throughout this time, Jewish nationalist discontent lay just beneath the surface, occasionally showing itself in the acts of sabotage and murder, finally erupting in the full scale insurrection of A.D. 66 which resulted in the siege and grisly destruction of Jerusalem in A.D. 70, described in such graphic detail by Josephus in books 5 and 6 of his History of the Jewish Wars against the Romans.

The sporadic local and sometimes empire-wide attempts by governments to extinguish the Christian church during the first century of her existence are another important part of the story, and will be touched upon briefly in the chapters dealing with the relationship between church and state.

This, briefly, is the context in which the words of Jesus were spoken and recorded. It was a time of great political unrest. Needless to say, political liberation movements thrived in this environment. Among the best known were the Zealots, a political-military organization of Jews committed to the struggle for Jewish liberty and independence. One of Jesus' disciples was a member of this group (Luke 6:15; Acts 1:13). More will be said about them later in this chapter.

What Jesus and his disciples taught and practised concerning love and forgiveness of enemies cannot be properly understood, appreciated or applied unless the volatile nationalistic milieu of which they were a part is taken into account. Given this context, it would be difficult to exaggerate the revolutionary nature of that love for enemies which they said would characterize true children of God! What follows is a summary of the New Testament teaching and record which makes it clear that participation in lethal violence is not a Christian option.

B. New Testament Teaching against Christian Participation in Lethal Violence

1. Jesus' teaching and life consistently demonstrated that right eous ends do not justify evil means.

a. He refused to secure the success of his mission by compromising with evil (Matthew 4:1-11; Mark 1:12-13; Luke 4:1-13).

b. He would not sanction the resisting of evil with evil (Matthew 5:38-42; Luke 6:29-30).

2. Jesus taught that the way of life and the way of love are inseparable. He did not advocate withdrawal from the "real world" of evil. Indeed, Jesus was accused of being too closely associated with evil (Matthew 11:19; Luke 7:34)! Instead of retreating from evil, Jesus went to the very heart of it, by his life, death and resurrection delivering a mortal blow to its very heart.

a. In the Beatitudes, the virtues he advocated are fundamentally incompatible with participation in lethal violence (Matthew 5:2-16).

b. The way of love requires love of one's racial foes and national enemies (Matthew 5:43-48; Luke 6:27-38; Romans 12:9, 17-21; 13:8-10; Galatians 5:14; James 2:8). The way of love, it must not be forgotten, is not passive, but active and practical (I Corinthians 13).

c. The way of love overcomes evil with good (Matthew 5:38-48; 7:12; Luke 6:27-38; Romans 12:17, 19-21; I Peter 3:9; I Thessalonians 5:15; Philippians 2:3-18). The one following the way of love is not guaranteed short-term happy consequences, but is linked eternally to the victorious Christ of the cross.

d. The way of love calls for arbitration, conciliation and unlimited forgiveness, rather than violence, in settling disputes (Matthew

5:23-25; 18:15-35).

 e. The way of love operates on the principle of forgiveness of one's enemies (Matthew 6:12; 18:21-22; Mark 11:25; Luke 17:3).

 3. Jesus forbade that which was inconsistent with the way of love for his would-be followers.

 a. He forbade killing, attempts to kill, and even the inner set of a person's mind that allowed killing (Matthew 5:21-22; 19:16-18).

 b. He forbade retaliatory reprisals (Matthew 5:38-39; 18:15-35).

 4. Jesus practised what he preached.

 a. He did not resist either his personal or his nation's enemies (Matthew 26:47-54; 27:27-31: Mark 14:60-65; 15:2-5).

 b. He forgave his enemies and loved them (Luke 23:34).

 c. He rebuked Peter for using the sword (Matthew 26:52).

 d. He refused kingship based on force (John 6:15).

 e. He accepted the cross, not because he had to, but because he chose to (Matthew 16:21-23).

 5. Jesus' followers are to practise what he preached and practised. We are not told to follow Jesus' carpentry, his rural, itinerant life, his teaching methods, or his celibacy; instead, we are told to emulate his servanthood (John 13:1-17; 15:20; 17:6-19); to share in his condescension (Philippians 2:3-14); to suffer with him (Philippians 3:10; II Corinthians 4:10; Colossians 1:24; I Corinthians 10:33; I Thessalonians 1:6); and to give up our lives as he did (Ephesians 5:1; I John 3:16-20).

 a. He required observance of the "golden rule" (Matthew 7:12).

 b. He proclaimed the law of love (Matthew 22:36-40).

 6. Christ's kingdom is not of this world. The source and nature of this kingdom is such that its subjects must never use physical violence in defending or expanding it (John 18:36; II Corinthians 10:4; Ephesians 6:10-20). If we are not to employ violence in propagating or defending that which we claim is most precious to us (our faith), is there anything worth killing for? "Where your treasure is, there your heart will be also" (Matthew 6:21).

 7. The Spirit of Christ is not of this world, and those who have been regenerated by and who possess that Spirit cannot use the methods of this world. Like Jesus, the followers of Jesus seek and save, rather than seek and destroy, the lost (Luke 9:55-56). The fruit of the Spirit is peace; those who possess the Spirit are peacemakers (Galatians 5:22; Matthew 5:9). Christians involved in the purpose of saving people's lives cannot pursue the deliberate practice of

destroying them. Life is that which people hold most precious, and the one who kills an unbeliever ensures that person's eternal physical and spiritual ruin.

8. Christ's methods are not of this world (II Corinthians 10:3-4; Ephesians 6:10-20).

9. Christ's values are not of this world. He and his followers see beneath the surface of things to the deeper levels of reality (Mark 8:35; John 12:25). If existence in this world is more important than life with Christ, then one belongs to this world, and will use the world's methods to save one's life . . . losing out both spiritually and physically as a result.

It is instructive to note that Peter's highly political confession, "You are the Christ" (Mark 8:29), elicited from his Messiah the surprising teaching on pacifism and the way of the cross! Peter's attempts to set Jesus straight resulted in the sternest rebuke Jesus ever gave to a disciple:"Out of my sight, Satan!" he said. "You do not have in mind the things of God, but the things of men" (Mark 8:33).

10. The Scriptures are clear on what it means to "love your neighbour as yourself." One cannot kill with love. Murder is a refusal to love. It is the opposite of forgiveness. One cannot kill and remain in fellowship with Christ anymore than one can remain in his fellowship while at the same time engaging in stealing, slandering, adultery, or deceit (John 15:10; I John 2:4; 3:12, 15; 4:8, 20).

Some have argued that it is possible to love the person you are killing. "Physical death," they argue, "is not as important as some of Jesus' disciples seem to think." Mark 9:42 is often cited, and the conclusion is drawn that if it is possible to hang a millstone around the neck of a sinner and cast him into the depths of the sea, it must be possible to act this way from love. This enemy can be killed without hating him, but actually loving him.

Such arguments are mere sophistry, the sort of deceptive reasoning that gave rise to the military crusades and religious inquisitions of the "Dark Ages." In the first place, the text is completely misused, since Jesus is describing the guilty person's standing in God's eyes, and is by no means encouraging his disciples to carry out such a judgement themselves! Furthermore, love in the Bible is never seen as an emotion independent of the actions which condition or express it. In the verse, "Love your neighbour as yourself," for example, can it be said that one who loves himself or herself could take his or her own life? Nor can you love your neighbour while at the same time killing him or her.

Or take as another example the verse, "Husbands, love your wives, just as Christ loved the church and gave himself up for her" (Ephesians 5:25). Can you conceive of a situation in which a husband might best express his love for his wife by killing her? Perhaps. But the Bible would call that sort of love murder. That which we love we cherish, rather than destroy.

11. The Scriptures are painfully clear on the significance God places upon love for an enemy. According to the gospel, the only really qualitative difference between Christian and non-Christian love is that Christian love, remarkably, includes enemies rather than just family and friends (Matthew 5:44; Luke 6:27-28; Romans 12:14)! There is nothing in the New Testament to suggest that there are exceptions to this rule.

12. The universality of the church only reinforces the case against Christian participation in war. In accepting the salvation which is in Christ Jesus, we are made members of the church, "which is his body." We are reconciled not only with God, but with brothers and sisters of like faith around the world (Galatians 3:27; Ephesians 2:13-18), regardless of race (Romans 10:12; Revelation 7:9), nationality (Colossians 3:11), or social situation (Galatians 3:28).

There is a single body (John 10:16; 11:52; I Corinthians 12:12; Ephesians 4:4-6; 2:19-22; Colossians 3:15). It is Christ's body, and all of the reconciled are members. Loyalty to Christ, and therefore to his body, transcends every other loyalty. Members of Christ's body cannot, therefore, take the carnal quarrels of persons to the point of destroying and thus desecrating the very body of Christ. If all Christians agreed not to kill Christians of other nations, that alone might prevent many wars.

13. There is nothing in the example of Christ and the apostles which suggests that it is right for their spiritual progeny to kill other human beings.

a. They always refused to fight, even when threatened with death. As far as we know, most of them died as martyrs.

b. They never initiated or participated in acts of lethal violence.

c. They didn't join the popular movement to liberate Palestine of that day. As was noted in the introduction to this chapter, Palestine was an oppressed land badly in need of liberation. Nor was there any shortage of men and women dedicated to the task of achieving political freedom for their beloved nation. Among the several militant groups organized around this cause, perhaps the best known was the Zealot party. Called "Zealots" because of their zeal for the law of God, this political liberation party was founded by Judas the Galilean, who led an unsuccessful revolt against Rome in A.D. 6. The Zealots opposed the payment of tribute to the pagan Roman emperor on the grounds that this constituted treason against God, Israel's true king.

The Zealots worked energetically to bring about a violent revolution. They were crushed in A.D. 6, but remained active underground, playing out one final tragic part in the drama for Jewish liberation in their epic, suicidal defence of their mountain fortress Masada against the Romans in A.D. 73.

Although one of his disciples was from the party of the Zealots, Jesus was not the military messiah they were looking for. Jesus did, it is true, proclaim the kingdom of God in a politically volatile context, but his kingdom agenda differed from that of the Zealots in several significant ways:

i. Jesus called for national repentance, rather than national resistance (Luke 13:3).

ii. Jesus saw peace as both the means and the end of the kingdom; accordingly, his followers were bidden to love their enemies (Matthew 5:43-48); the Zealots, on the other hand, regarded war as the means, and peace as the end; hatred for national enemies was the fuel of their nationalist cause.

iii. Jesus identified himself with the suffering servant, and called upon his followers to suffer (Luke 9:22-24, 44); the Zealots, in contrast, deeply resented the suffering being inflicted on their nation, and called upon fellow Jews to revolt.

iv. Jesus responded to Roman domination by extending the grace of the gospel to all people, even the enemy! The Zealots had a vision of God that was narrow, parochial, tribal.

C. Questions for Discussion

1. After an examination of the references cited under each subpoint in section B above, discuss and illustrate from contemporary life the differences, in theory and practice, between the wisdom of Jesus and the conventional wisdom of the world on the use of lethal violence to either prevent or avenge evil.

2. What relevance does the teaching have for Christians in (a) times of peace and (b) in times of war?

3. What might be some of the personal and family costs of following Jesus' way of love in situations where all of society calls out for violent retaliation against a personal or national aggressor?

4. How can we as parents teach the way of love to our children?

Chapter 6
The Old Testament Sanction of War

A. The Problem

If it is difficult to find New Testament sanction for Christian participation in lethal violence, it is at least as difficult to find support for pacifism in the Old Testament. The contrast between the two Testaments is truly striking. In the New Testament, on the one hand, Christ's followers are characterized by a quality of unconditional love which makes violence, even against mortal enemies, unthinkable. In the Old Testament, on the other hand, the whole climate frequently breathes violence of the most brutal kind imaginable. For example:

1. It provides, in gruesome detail, descriptions of genocidal massacres carried out by God's people at God's command (Numbers 31:1-54; Deuteronomy 20:1-20; Joshua 6:16-24; 8:1-29; 10:1-43; Judges 21:1-25; I Samuel 15:1-35).

2. The three Old Testament heroes of faith most frequently mentioned in the Gospels never hesitated to shed blood, often in a most brutal manner. Moses had three thousand men slaughtered for having worshipped the golden calf (Exodus 32:25-29); David spent much of his time making war, and killed almost the entire household of Nabal because the latter had doubted his loyalty to Saul (I Samuel 25); Elijah had four hundred prophets of Baal chopped to pieces after their spectacular defeat on Mount Carmel (I Kings 18).

3. The Psalms themselves are studded with cruel invective, ugly curses, and outspoken lust for terrible revenge upon enemies (e.g., Psalm 69:22-28; 109; 137:7-9; 139:19-22).

The Old Testament does not seem to manifest the gentleness and kindness towards all creatures of God and forgiving love of enemies, which so characterize the New Testament. In the Old Testament, God is portrayed as leading people in war, sometimes ordering them not to take any prisoners but to kill all who were captured. How then, can war be forbidden for God's people now?

It is helpful to remember that the relationship between the Old and New Testaments is a problem which has challenged and perplexed students of the Scriptures since the earliest days of the church. While Christian theologians are deeply divided in their answers to many of the apparent dilemmas that separate the two Testaments, there has always been general agreement on three important points: (a) Much in the Old Testament that is descriptive of or even prescriptive for God's people then, is not normative for the people of God today; (b) it is the life of faithful obedience to God that characterizes and unites both Old Testament and New Testament believers (Hebrews 10:26-12:3); and (c) Christ is the central and unifying theme of both Testaments (Matthew 5:17; Luke 24:27,44; John 5:39; Hebrews 10:7). (For a study of this important point, see *Christ: The Theme of the Bible* by Norman Geisler. Chicago:Moody Press, 1968).

B. Proposed Solutions to the Problem

Attempts to reconcile the apparent contradictions between the Old and New Testaments tend to follow one of three possible lines of reasoning:

1. Yahweh of the Old Testament and God the Father revealed in the New Testament are two different Gods. This was the view of Marcion, a gnostic who lived during the second century. He rejected the God of the Old Testament together with God's wars, arguing that this God could not be the Father of Jesus Christ. He wrote a book, *Antitheses,* in which he developed his thesis of a complete and absolute distinction between Christianity and Judaism. In his book he contrasted contradictory statements from the law and the gospel. In the name of Christian love, he rejected the God who had destroyed the human race with the flood, consumed Sodom and Gomorrah with fire, plagued the Egyptians, hardened Pharaoh's heart, blessed the murderer Moses and the ruthless warrior Joshua, and had the children who mocked Elisha devoured by bears. Had not the God of the New Testament inspired Paul to write, "Let not the sun go down upon your wrath?" Yet the God of the Old Testament had helped Joshua keep the sun up until his wrath went down. Jesus was gentle and meek of heart, concerned about sparing the life even of an adulterous woman. In the Old Testament, life seems cheap, with even the most devoted of God's followers apparently feeling no scruples about shedding blood; but in the New Testament, life is precious, and even enemies are

not to be resisted.

Marcion was excommunicated from the Church in A.D. 144. He was a pacifist, but a gnostic and, therefore, a heretic. No believer in one God could ever accept his teaching. Gnostics taught that the world is fundamentally evil because it contains wars, flies, fleas, and fevers. The body was a prison from which the spirit had to be liberated. Salvation (liberation from the clutches of matter) came by means of knowledge (*gnosis*).

2. A second way of resolving the difficulty lay in seeing the wars of the Old Testament as holy wars based on God's covenant with a chosen people. This covenant is superseded when the new covenant begins. God's covenant with Israel promised protection and provision in return for obedience. God would be their Lord, Leader, Protector. They would not protect themselves, nor decide by themselves whether or when or how to conduct a war. All this would be done by Yahweh . . . God's part in the covenant. If Israel failed to abide by their part of the covenant, they would be defeated (Exodus 19; Leviticus 26).

An example of this may be found in the story of the exodus from Egypt, when the Israelites found themselves trapped between Pharaoh's army and the Red Sea; they complained (Exodus 14:11-12); Moses replied (Exodus 14:13-14). God's relationship with the chosen people is clearly seen in Moses' message:

> Do not be afraid. Stand firm and you will see the deliverance the Lord will bring today. The Egyptians you see today you will never see again. The Lord will fight for you; you need only to be still.

Israel was never free to make war or take life on the volition of her leaders alone . . . whether prophet, judge, or king (e.g., II Chronicles 18-20). If there was a question of war, Yahweh was to be consulted. Yahweh, through the prophets, could approve or disapprove of a given war, and could lay down the conditions under which it was to be fought.

Frequently, God would punish the people by allowing them to be conquered and taken into captivity. Armed resistance on such occasions was as futile as any resistance against God must necessarily be. To take up arms in obedience to the state in such instances was to take up arms against God himself. Assyria conquered the Northern Kingdom in 722 B.C. in accordance with the prediction of Jeremiah and Isaiah (Jeremiah 5:12-17; Isaiah 10:5-6; 45:1-6; 43:8-

13; 42:1-4; 31:1; 53). The Southern Kingdom continued, but only as a vassal of Assyria. Then in 587 B.C. Judah fell to the Babylonians, and most of the leaders were taken into exile. From this time until 1948, except for the brief one hundred year period under the Maccabees (164 B.C. — 63 B.C.), God's people ceased to exist as an autonomous political entity.

Throughout this time, God's prophets were given the task of putting the disaster into perspective. They forced the people to take a second look at their conquest history, just as we are now taking a second look at how our ancestors settled the land at the expense of the native peoples. Isaiah tried to impress upon his readers three important conclusions:

a. Israel had to relearn what it meant to be God's "chosen people." They had to learn the hard way that they were not the only people God could use to achieve God's purposes (Isaiah 10:5-6). God could use the brutal Assyrians; God could call the pagan conqueror Cyrus, "my anointed," a notion as preposterous and unpopular at the time as would be a modern preacher's reference to the Ayatollah Khomeini as God's chosen one today (Isaiah 45:1-7; 44:28)!

b. Israel was specially chosen in order to reveal God to the nations. God was no mere tribal or national deity, but the God of all nations. It was Israel's mandate to faithfully demonstrate and proclaim this fact (Isaiah 42:1-7; 43:8-13).

c. Israel's special calling to reveal God to other nations would not be accomplished by defeating them in battle, but by becoming the suffering servant of the nations (Isaiah 31:1; 42:1-7). Out of painful obedience would come great benefit for all nations.

As Susan Steiner points out in her book, *Joining the Army that Sheds No Blood* (Scottdale, PA: Herald Press, 1982), "... Israel as a 'powerful' military nation is not the Old Testament's last word." The strong, united kingdom of Saul, David, and Solomon lasted only one century before entering a period of unbroken decline. It is important to remember that throughout most of the Old Testament, God did not work through a mighty military power until the moment of Jesus' birth, when God suddenly switched strategies to the foolishness of the cross and the weakness of the church (Steiner, pp. 93-95).

However one may try to justify Christian participation in the lethal violence of contemporary nations by citing Old Testament violence as a normative, prescriptive precedent, it must be acknowledged that few nations today fight "holy wars" in the same manner required of God's people in the Old Testament. In the first place, those who advocate just wars (of defense) have tended to avoid the awkward question of whether or not they deserved to be defeated . . . whether, in fact, their nation's mortal enemy might not be God's scourge, against whom resistance would be as presumptuous as it would be futile. Secondly, how many modern "Christian" nations would accept the conditions imposed by God in some of the holy wars of that day? Is it really possible to imagine President Reagan announcing that God has promised victory for the United States over the USSR, on the condition that the US do away with all conventional and nuclear weapons, dismiss all but three hundred servicemen, and equip these soldiers to fight with only horns, pitchers, and torches?

This was the way in which the holy war operated. The enemy and the conditions of the war were set by God, so that there could be absolutely no doubt that victory was due to God rather than to military strength and strategic alliances (See Richard McSorley, *New Testament Basis of Peacemaking*, pp. 56-63).

A third series of questions needs to be answered by those who appeal to the Old Testament examples of war to justify Christian participation in their nation's wars: Just who are God's chosen people today? Where are they? Should they go to war? Against whom? If it is agreed that God's chosen ones today are members of the church, which is Christ's body, and if we say that this chosen people is not a local or a national entity, but a universal, international phenomenon, then are we forced to argue that the Church should take up arms and engage in crusades and holy wars? There is no biblical support for this notion.

3. A third way of dealing with the dilemma is more theologically and practically satisfactory. The New Testament fulfills the Old Testament. The idea of extension or enlargement is crucial to any understanding of the relationship between the pacifism of the New Testament and the wars of the Old Testament.

The Bible itself indicates that God's revelation to humankind was progressive. That is, God's own initiative brought people up ". . . through the theological infancy of the Old Testament to the maturity of the New Testament" (See Bernard Ramm, *Protestant Biblical Interpretation: A Textbook of Hermeneutics.* Grand Rapids: Baker, 1970. pp. 102-104).

In his Sermon on the Mount, for example, Jesus did not tell his disciples to break the law, for as he pointed out, he himself had come to fulfill (i.e., fill the law full) the law (Matthew 5:17-48). Christ came to bring out the deeper, more elemental significance of the law. The law was good, as far as it went, but it did not go far enough. Thus, while it taught that murder is wrong, Jesus taught that even to think of murder or be angry with a brother or sister is condemned (Matthew 5:22). In the Old Testament adultery is wrong; in the New Testament even contemplation of adultery is forbidden. If "an eye for an eye and a tooth for a tooth" was taught in the Old Testament law, Jesus taught that evil persons should not be violently resisted. If the law taught that neighbours should be loved and enemies should be hated, Christ taught that even enemies, especially enemies, were to be the objects of his followers' agape love.

In his Epistle to the Galatians, Paul distinguishes between God's dealings before Christ came and after Christ came. The pre-Christ era is referred to by Paul as the period of childhood and immaturity. The Old Testament covers the period of theological kindergarten. In Christ the fullness of revelation comes, and God's sons are reckoned as mature heirs.

The same point is made in Hebrews 1:1-2, where we read that God has two great revelations, one of which was given through the prophets to Israel, the other to the church through God's Son. The author goes on to explain throughout the book that the Old Testament revelation was a material revelation, with spiritual truth being encased in cultural forms; it was a revelation of types, shadows, and parables. But the New Testament is a spiritual revelation, containing the substance, reality, and fulfillment of the Old Covenant forms.

An understanding of progressive revelation is very important for anyone attempting to harmonize the Old and the New Testaments. We expect a more complete revelation of God in the New Testament. This does not mean that the teaching of the Old Testament is not clear or valid. It does mean that the heart of Christian belief and practice is to be found in the New Testament which contains the clearer revelation of God. It is in the light of Christ's life and teaching that his followers should interpret the Old Testament, and not vice versa.

It is not difficult for most Christians to understand that the Old Testament prohibition of the eating of pork does not apply under the New Covenant. Nor should we bridle at the discovery that war is

52

no longer a part of God's missionary strategy for his people.

C. Some Conclusions

From the foregoing discussion on the relationship of the sanction of war in the Old Testament and the practice of Christians in the 20th century, three conclusions may be drawn:

1. The wars of the Old Testament cannot be used to defend Christian participation in the wars of today. Many practices encouraged among the people of the Old Covenant, such as the killing of witches (Exodus 22:18), the owning of slaves (Leviticus 25:44), the execution of stubborn sons (Deuteronomy 21:18-21), the stoning of adulterers (Deuteronomy 22:22-24), the isolation of menstruating women (Leviticus 15:19-31), no longer pertain to the people of the New Covenant. So it is with war. Jesus did not come as a warrior, and he does not live on earth now in his body which is the church as one who seeks and destroys his enemies. When Jesus was and is moved to act in the cause of justice, he shed and he sheds his own blood, not the blood of his enemies or unjust oppressors. In this way he identifies himself with both the persecuted and the persecutor. It is the foolishness of the cross, not the power of an army, which overcomes the forces of evil.

2. God as the author of life, has power over life and death. All who have ever lived have received the gift of life from God; all except two (Enoch and Elijah) who have ever lived have had or will have this gift of life taken from them in due course. Life is a stewardship, something held in trust. It belongs to God, ultimately. It is precisely because all of life belongs to God that God can forbid people from taking it.

3. The common thread uniting the Old Covenant and the New Covenant people of God is faithful obedience to God. When God in Old Testament times directed the people to take life, the person acting in obedience to God was right to take life. But whose life shall the obedient child of God take today? And at whose behest? The New Testament is clear: obedience to God today means refraining from taking life. It means proclaiming through life and word the Good News of the mercy and forgiveness and love of God through Jesus Christ.

It is sobering to realize that obedience to God may one day involve Christ's followers in the awesome violence of the judgements described in the book of Revelation (chapters 14-20). But for now, the way of lethal violence is not the way of Christ. We can die, but we cannot kill, in Jesus' name. The way of the cross may appear to be foolish, but it is actually the very power of God. And the way of the cross is not optional for Christ's followers (I Corinthians 1:17-18; Galatians 6:12-14; Ephesians 2:14; Mark 8:34; Philippians 3:7-21).

D. Questions for Discussion

1. Study the following passages with a view to determining the nature and extent and by what criteria a Christian should limit his or her obedience to the "state."
Mark 12:13-17; Romans 13:1-10; I Peter 2:11-25

2. How can one resolve the apparent conflict between God as revealed in the Old Testament and God as revealed through Christ in the New Testament? In formulating your answers to this question, study and compare the following Old Testament and New Testament passages:

a. Old Testament	b. New Testament
Numbers 31:1-54	Matthew 5:38-48
Deuteronomy 20:1-20	John 3:16
Joshua 8:1-29	I Corinthians 13:1-13
Joshua 10:1-43	James 4:1-10
Judges 21:1-25	I John 2:15-17
I Samuel 15:1-35	I John 3:11-20
Exodus 23:20-33	I John 4:7-21
Deuteronomy 2:26-35	I John 5:19
Deuteronomy 3:1-11	
Joshua 6:15-21	

3. In your opinion, would it be possible for someone obeying the will of God as revealed in the above Old Testament passages to simultaneously obey God's will as revealed in the New Testament? If not, how do you resolve the apparent contradiction between the differing revelations of God's nature and will? If so, explain how.

Chapter 7
Christians and the State

A. The Problem

Those who argue that Christians not only may but must, in certain circumstances, take up arms and engage in the destruction of enemies usually argue along the following lines:

> Of course, the follower of Christ must be non-violent in his or her private life. God has commissioned the church to proclaim the gospel, and it is clear that the church has no right to resort to the sword in persuading people to become Christians. But God has also commissioned the state to keep order, and has commanded Christians to be in subjection to its authority. Since God has granted to states the right to use the sword, Christian participation in war or mortal violence in obedience to the state constitutes obedience to God.

B. The Biblical Data

A number of New Testament texts are employed by those who argue for a Christian's active participation in his or her country's wars. A number of these were discussed in the lesson "The New Testament's Apparent Sanction of Violence" (Chapter 4). Of these, three in particular address the question of the relationship between the Christian and the state:Romans 13:1-7; I Peter 2:13-17; Titus 3:1.

> Everyone must submit himself to the governing authorities, for there is no authority except that which God has established. The authorities that exist have been established by God. Consequently, he who rebels against the authority is rebelling against what God has instituted, and those who do so will bring judgement on themselves. For rulers hold no terror for those who do right, but for those who do wrong. Do you want to be free from fear of the one in authority? Then do what is right and he will commend you. For he is God's servant to do

good. But if you do wrong, be afraid, for he does not
bear the sword for nothing. He is God's servant, an agent
of wrath to bring punishment on the wrongdoer. Therefore, it is necessary to submit to the authorities, not only
because of possible punishment but also because of
conscience. This is why you pay taxes, for the authorities
are God's servants, who give their full time to governing.
Give everyone what you owe him: If you owe taxes, pay
taxes; if revenue, then revenue; if respect, then respect;
if honor, then honor (Romans 13:1-7, NIV).

This text was written around A.D. 57. Paul's first imprisonment
and trial under Nero, and his subsequent acquittal must have
influenced his views (See Acts 24-28).

Submit yourselves for the Lord's sake to every authority
instituted among men: whether to the king, as to the
supreme authority, or to governors, who are sent by him
to punish those who do wrong and to commend those
who do right. For it is God's will that by doing good you
should silence the ignorant talk of foolish men. Live as
free men; but do not use your freedom as a coverup for
evil; live as servants of God. Show proper respect to
everyone: Love the brotherhood of believers, fear God,
honor the king (I Peter 2:13-17, NIV).

Peter wrote these words sometime in A.D. 63 — A.D. 64, just
before the terrible Neronian persecution.

Remind the people to be subject to rulers and authorities, to be obedient, to be ready to do whatever is good..
. (Titus 3:1, NIV).

This advice from Paul comes just after the outbreak of Nero's
attempt to obliterate the church, at a time when to confess Christ
was to commit a capital crime.

C. What These Texts Teach Regarding Christian Attitudes to the State

1. Typical Post-Constantinian Understanding

Most theologians since the time of Constantine have argued that
God has given to the state a two-fold mission: (a) to protect and
maintain religion and morality, and (b) to protect and ensure social
order. This was the view of both Luther and Calvin, who regarded

the state as the protector of religion, morals and society. Both of these men operated in a form of theocratic state, presided over by "Christian" rulers. To some degree, therefore, since church and state were intertwined, and all religion was civil religion, this understanding seemed to make sense.

With the advent of the purely secular state this past century, theologians found it necessary to update this traditional view, by modifying it slightly. According to many contemporary theologians such as Karl Barth, Reinhold Niebuhr and Robert Culver, the state's mission, whether it knows it or not, is to enable the church to carry out its task of preaching the gospel by ensuring social order. The liberty of the church is guaranteed by the state; the state's existence is guaranteed by the prayers of the church. This understanding is based upon Paul's words in I Timothy 2:2-4, where it is asked that prayers be made

> for kings and all those in authority, that we may live peaceful and quiet lives in all godliness and holiness. This is good, and pleases God our Saviour, who wants all men to be saved and to come to a knowledge of the truth.

Most theological advocacy of Christian participation in lethal violence seems to rest on five propositions:

a. God has commissioned the church to preach the gospel.

b. God has commissioned the state to ensure order and prevent anarchy.

c. Every Christian is both a member of the church and a citizen of a nation.

d. As a Christian one must obey God by living according to the ethical teaching of the New Testament.

e. As a citizen one must obey God by conforming to the demands of the state, where these do not clearly conflict with the gospel.

According to this view, one glorifies God by obeying the gospel ethic in private life, and by abiding by the state ethic in civil life. While there is a good deal of practical sense in this popular understanding of the two spheres, the Christian needs to ask a number of questions of this traditional understanding.

2. Questioning the Post-Constantine View

a. If God has ordained that the state should ensure order in society, what is the Christian's response to be toward those states which seem to establish and perpetuate disorder? The traditional view seems naively optimistic about human nature in this case. This is strange, since most who hold to this position today insist on the sinfulness of individuals. What basis is there to believe that the state is "naturally good"?

b. How can it be that the ethical and moral demands of the gospel are one thing for private life, and another thing for civil life? May Christians ever temporarily suspend gospel morality provided they have instructions from the state to do so? Are Christians to be morally schizophrenic, finding it normal to kill and lie when the state requires it, while protesting virtuously against such practices in private life?

c. The idea of a dual standard of morality seems inconsistent with biblical teaching. In effect it would mean that God asks me as a Canadian citizen to kill the enemy soldiers who invade my country, and as a member of the church to welcome them by proclaiming the Good News to them, feeding them if they are hungry, sheltering them if they are exposed, and loving them. This is obviously impossible; such "duties" are absolutely contradictory. It is not possible to obey God by disobeying God. Two contradictory orders cannot both be from God. God cannot ask me as a citizen to do the opposite of what would be required of me as a member of the church.

d. Can the state, even the secular state, really be morally autonomous? Can it do whatever it likes in the sphere of moral and social life, compelling its citizens to obey orders which in private life would be clearly immoral for the Christian? Has the state the right to use any violence, including gas chambers, atomic bombs, torture and genocide? If not, what is the basis of the Christian's critique? If it is the Scriptures, then we do not have a dual morality, one for the church and one for the state. Both church and state will be judged by the same Lord.

e. In what circumstances does the Christian have an obligation to refuse to obey the state, and even resist it? In theory, no Christian would argue that obedience to the state is absolute and uncondi- tional. Any doctrine of unconditional obedience to the state cannot be reconciled with the doctrine of God's sovereignty. There cannot be two absolute sovereigns. One must, where there is a contradic- tion, obey God rather than persons.

But how shall the Christian know when he or she has an obliga- tion to disobey the state? Traditional theology gives the state the benefit of the doubt: "If in doubt, obey." But since there will almost always be doubt, there will almost always be obedience. The most terrible crimes committed by persons on behalf of the state, from the Inquisition to Auschwitz to Hiroshima, have been rationalized on the principle that in the event of doubt, you must trust the authority, which takes responsibility for the order. The Ethiopian soldier who is ordered by his superiors to ignite the kerosene-soaked Christian "enemy of the state"; the Russian pilot whose commander instructs him to napalm the Afghanistani village; the American navy flier whose orders are to bomb a family residence in Libya; each of these soldiers justifies his action on the grounds that someone else made him do it.

3. An Alternative Understanding

What exactly is the nature of submission to which Christians are called (Romans 13:1,5; Titus 3:1; I Peter 2:13)?

a. These texts clearly teach that all authorities which exist in human society, including political authorities, are taken very seriously by God and have a real and positive role to play in God's overall plan. It is, therefore, "for the Lord's sake" that we must submit obediently to them.

b. Christians are to submit to and obey all authorities placed above them, not only political authorities. Thus slaves are to obey their masters (Titus 2:9; Ephesians 6:5; Colossians 3:22; I Peter 2:18); wives are to submit to their husbands (I Corinthians 14:34; Ephesians 5:22; Colossians 3:18; I Timothy 2:11; Titus 2:5; I Peter 3:1); the young are to submit to elders (Ephesians 6:1; Colossians 3:20; I Timothy 3:4; I Peter 5:5); Christians are to submit to their spiritual leaders (I Thessalonians 5:12; Hebrews 13:17); and citizens are to submit to their kings and governors.

c. Submission in these contexts does not imply passive obedience to all instructions. Peter and Paul both suffered execution for their disobedience to the king. There is an active spiritual dimension to this submission involving three vital elements: (i) intercessory prayer for those in authority over us, that they may be faithful and just in fulfilling their mandate (I Timothy 2:2); (ii) faithful witness of our faith to these masters; (iii) suffering, since these authorities to whom Christians are called to submit are not necessarily or naturally just. This is true for slaves in particular (I Peter 2:18-20), but also for all Christians in general who are faithful to their primary calling. Such suffering must be endured patiently, though not passively, since prayer and witness are not passive activities.

d. The call to submit to the state comes in the context of apostolic teaching on mutual submission (Ephesians 5:21) and submission toward whoever wields authority among persons. Far too frequently, the texts on submission to the state are detached from their contexts and then used to argue for a more or less unconditional obedience to the state. But in all cases, the context shows that the issue is not that of passive obedience, but of love, suffering and meekness. It must not be forgotten that the call to submission is addressed to people who are, in fact, oppressed and persecuted. It is these people who are asked to pray, suffer and witness by their meekness and their faith. Because of the example of Jesus, and because of his continuing life through his church, Christians are called upon to suffer. They are never called upon to inflict suffering.

e. Each of the texts on submission must be understood in the light of its context; and in all three cases the context speaks of unconditional love of both neighbour and enemy. Submission to authorities is not a license to kill, but an integral part of loving our neighbour. Thus, the Romans 13 passage is preceded and followed by admonitions to unconditional and unlimited love (Romans 12:9-21; 13:8-10); Titus 3:1 occurs in the context of exhortations to moderation, patience, love, peacefulness, gentleness and meekness towards all persons; I Peter 2:13-17 likewise occurs in the context of Christian behaviour which is distinctly Christlike (I Peter 2:11-12; 18-5:11).

f. The letter to the Romans was written in A.D. 57, seven years before the first great persecution of the church by the Roman Empire. Christians at this time were barely tolerated, and it is not unlikely that, like all such loathed minorities, those in Rome were tempted to contemptuous disregard of the state. Paul outlines the biblical doctrine of submission to authority, although he says nothing about Christians taking up the sword on behalf of the state. Acknowledging and submitting to the general authority of the state is one thing; obeying every specific demand of the state is quite another. When the state commands something against God's will for the believer, the believer must disobey (Acts 5:29).

g. Several years later, Rome burned. Christians were blamed for setting the fire, and a general persecution of Christians throughout the Empire was initiated by imperial edict. It is interesting to note that the New Testament letters written after the fire depict the state in quite a different light. In the book of Revelation (thought to have been written sometime around A.D. 68 — A.D. 69 at the height of the Neronian persecution, or between A.D. 95 — A.D. 96 during the empire-wide persecution of Domitian), Rome is described as the instrument and embodiment of the devil. "That great city, which reigns over the kings of the earth" (Revelation 17:18), seated on the seven mountains (v.9), and upon "the waters" which are "peoples and multitudes and nations and tongues" (v.15) clearly refers to the imperial capital of the Empire, Rome itself.

In the mystery of God's providence, both Satan and Rome are useful to God's purposes. Job is certainly not obliged to obey Satan (Job 1:6-8)! John, "the disciple whom Jesus loved," discloses another side of the Christian attitude to the state, a side not evident in Romans 13, but suggested in I Peter 2-5 and in Revelation. As one who has suffered and observed suffering of Christians at the instigation of the state, John scorns Rome's famous compromise with "the kings of the earth" who "lived sensuously with her" (18:9); he catalogues the sumptuous traffic (vv. 12-13) of the "merchants of the earth who have become rich by the wealth of her sensuality" (v. 3); he stigmatizes the artistic brilliance of a city and empire (v.22) already "drunk with the blood of the saints and with the blood of the witnesses of Jesus" (17:6; 18:24). In short, Rome is the chief agent of the anti-Christian "beast that comes up out of the abyss" and makes war on God's people (11:7).

h. Since the time of Constantine, Christians have tended to think that if a state no longer persecutes the church, that is a sure sign of its being a just state. But this is not necessarily a valid conclusion. It is equally possible that the state is really empowered by Satan and his system, but that it does not persecute the lukewarm church which grants it all it wants.

It is clear that, at the very least, the state may become dominated by the Dragon, demanding state-worship, fighting with the saints, blaspheming God, the Beast of the Abyss from Revelation 13, ruling the whole world. It can become a demonic power, vainly trying to escape from the sovereignty of Christ.

It is also possible to conclude that all states since the time of Christ tend to be demonic. A number of texts in the New Testament refer to "higher powers . . . which come from God." It is said that these authorities, powers, or dominions have been created in Christ, by him, and for him (Colossians 1:16); but disregarding the wisdom of God, they have crucified the Lord (I Corinthians 2:8; cf.

Luke 22-53). But Christ has triumphed over them by the cross and has despoiled them (Colossians 2:15). Since his resurrection he, as the head of them (Colossians 2:10), sits enthroned above them (Ephesians 1:20,21). Since that day they have been subject to him (I Peter 3:22), but the church by the foolishness of preaching must reveal to them the wisdom of God (Ephesians 6:12); for in their rebellion they continue to fight against Christ (Romans 8:38-39; cf.Luke 12:1). Christ's church must arm itself with all the weapons of God in order to strive against them (Ephesians 6:10-20). They will finally be destroyed and rendered powerless in the day of Christ (I Corinthians 2:6; 15:24). In all of this there is no question of collaboration between the church and the powers; there is only a mortal spiritual struggle in which Christians are often martyred (Revelation 13:7).

It seems that in North American Protestant theology, Romans 13 has all but eclipsed Ephesians 6:12. The early Christians actually lived within the terrible struggle depicted in Ephesians 6:12. Almost all the New Testament heroes were imprisoned, tortured or condemned to death. Many of Christ's followers around the world continue to suffer the persecution that Christ promised would be the lot of his true disciples (John 15:18-25; Matthew 5:10-12). Estimates on the total number of Christians who will be martyred for their faith in 1988 run as high as 310,000 (David Barrett, *International Bulletin of Missionary Research*, January 1988). In Africa alone, over 25,000 Christians are known to be imprisoned under terrible conditions, charged with the crime of being Christian (*Moody Monthly*, May 1986, p. 100).

For comfort-loving contemporary western Christians, Christ's ominous words are not merely incomprehensible, but mistaken. And Paul's foreboding words in Ephesians 6 concerning the Christian's struggle against the authorities and powers of this dark world have been, practically speaking, modified to reflect the western church's compromise with the state; "Obey the rulers, the authorities, and the powers of this dark world without question, serving them faithfully, even laying down your lives on their behalf. For our struggle is against flesh and blood, and the weapons of our warfare are carnal, not spiritual."

D. Questions for Discussion
Discuss a biblical response to the following objections to pacifism:

1. The gospel cannot be applied directly to people living within modern states. The gospel can only be a norm to discriminate between the lesser of two evils, a guide to show us how far away we are from the ideal. It cannot be used as a direct guide for us in deciding for or against participation in a war.

2. People are sinful and incapable of living by the love ethic of Jesus. War is necessary because social and international order is based upon balance of power. Sinners need not only coaxing, but coercion.

3. Gospel morality is concerned with my personal relationships, not with international relationships. The state is not bound by gospel morality.

4. A nation has the right and the obligation to defend itself.

5. There are situations in which the defense of loved ones requires violence.

6. Communists could invade our country.

7. Pacifism is not practical. It cannot work in the real world. It is naive and simplistic.

8. Spiritual and human values are worth more than life, and must, if need be, be gained or defended by war.

9. Pacifists are cowards. They let someone else do the fighting and take the risks, while they happily reap the resulting benefits.

10. Lethal violence works as a deterrent to evil.

E. For Further Reading

Bainton, Roland H. *Christian Attitudes toward War and Peace.* (Chapter 10). Nashville: Abingdon Press, 1960.

Hershberger, Guy Franklin. *War, Peace, and Nonresistance.* (Chapter 8). Scottdale: Herald Press, 1969.

Lasserre, Jean. *War and the Gospel.* (Part III). London: James Clarke & Co., 1962.

McSorley, Richard. *New Testament Basis of Peacemaking.* (Chapter 2). Scottdale: Herald Press, 1985.

Chapter 8
Representative Christian Teaching
on Church and State

The sixteenth and seventeenth centuries, usually referred to as the Reformation period of church history, were marked by violent religious wars. At that time, current understanding of the proper relationship between Christians and the state tended to fit into one of five different categories: Roman Catholic, Calvinist, Lutheran, Quaker, or Anabaptist (See Arthur Holmes, ed., *War and Christian Ethics*. Grand Rapids: Baker, 1975, pp. 140-189). Holmes classifies Christian views on the subject into four broad categories: Lutheran, Calvinist, Catholic, and Anabaptist. Roland Bainton sees a fifth distinctive category in the Quaker view of church and state. See his book, *Christian Attitudes toward War and Peace*. Nashville: Abingdon, 1960, pp. 136-172).

A. Roman Catholic

Roman Catholics believed in two distinct standards of Christian behaviour: one for ordinary believers and one for the clergy. The Christian ethic which applied to the masses was not unduly rigorous, and scarcely raised the question of whether or not ordinary Catholics should or should not be involved in the running of the state and participate in all forms of state-sanctioned violence. The clergy, on the other hand, were committed to a more strict ethic which required, to a greater or lesser extent, that they withdraw from sins and necessary compromises of larger Christendom. The pope could, and frequently did, wield two swords:the spiritual sword of the Word over the church, and the secular sword of steel over unbelievers.

B. Calvinist

While Calvinists stressed the total depravity of human nature, they also believed in an infinitely sovereign God who, electing some people to eternal life, graciously brought them to repentance and faith by means of the Holy Spirit. It is the mandate of these redeemed ones to tackle the problems of living in a fallen world, with a view to ultimately creating a Christian society in which the Christian ethic would be imposed upon the non-elect by laws enforced by Christian magistrates and police. The city of Geneva, as well as the Puritan settlements of New England, operated on this principle.

C. Lutheran

Lutherans saw no possibility of a "Christian society." They understood the church to be commissioned by God to proclaim the good news of reconciliation through Christ, and they regarded the church to be the community of those who, by faith, have been saved and who, in their private lives, practice the gospel ethic. On the other hand, the state had also been commissioned by God, and had to, of necessity use violence in dealing with fallen persons. Accordingly, the Christian as a citizen was not only justified but obligated to undertake his or her share of unpleasant tasks made necessary for the state by the fact of human sinfulness.

D. Quaker

Quakers, formally known as the Society of Friends, were opposed to war, and did not believe that the state should interfere with the church. While refusing to participate in war, they took an active part in politics, believing that the radical Christian ethic of the Sermon on the Mount was not incompatible with Romans 13. William Penn's "holy experiment" in government, begun in Pennsylvania in 1682, is the best known attempt to apply the pacifist ways of the New Testament to government. Penn envisioned a government without an army or a navy, and foresaw the day when the police and jails would also be unnecessary.

This outlook was made possible by the Quakers' hopeful outlook for the world. In response to a critic who described the Quaker view of the state as fit only for "a world on the moon," one Quaker retorted:

> After a long night of apostasy, the spirit of Christ is awakening again and gathering men together to the true Church, making them pure and peaceable. As the Lord does this so will it go on, and the nations, kings, princes, great ones, as this principle is raised in them, and the contrary wisdom, the earthly policy (which undoes all) brought down, so will they feel the blessings of God in

themselves, and become a blessing to others (Bainton, p. 163).

As a matter of historical record, the Pennsylvania experiment failed. While it might have succeeded if all citizens had been Quaker, in fact it was a mixed society, comprised not only of Quakers, Mennonites, Dunkers, and Moravians (all of whom were pacifist), but of Scotch Presbyterians who had no part in pacifism. Furthermore, Pennsylvania belonged to the British state which required support of military operations. The Quakers discovered that it was not possible in a mixed society for pacifists to wield the sword for the government without losing their pacifist beliefs. Pressure to participate in the French and Indian War of 1756 resulted in the resignation of many Quakers from the government. (For other Quaker experiments, see Bainton, pp. 157-172, and Hershberger, pp. 158-160).

E. Anabaptist

Anabaptists make a sharp distinction between the kingdom of this world and the kingdom of Christ. The kingdom of this world is comprised of those who, because they are unregenerated, live according to the lusts of the flesh. To restrain fallen persons from preying upon each other, God instituted the state, endowing it with the coercive power of the sword.

The kingdom of Christ, by way of contrast, is not of this world. Comprised only of those who have been born again as new creatures and who will not avenge themselves, this kingdom is characterized by love and meekness. In the words of Menno Simons,

> Our fortress is Christ, our defense is patience, our sword is the Word of God, and our victory is the sincere, firm, unfeigned faith in Jesus Christ. Spears and swords of iron we will leave to those who, alas, consider human blood and swine's blood well-nigh of equal value (Bainton, p. 153).

Confronted by examples of Old Testament warriors approved by God, Anabaptists replied that the New Testament represented a radical new order under Christ, and that this order superseded that of the Old Testament. Jesus' kingdom was based on the Sermon on the Mount, and his instructions were to be literally obeyed by his followers. Striving to restore Christianity to the pristine purity of the pre-Constantinian era, Anabaptists engaged in aggressive missionary activity, believing that the gathering of the pure bride of Christ was a necessary prelude to the return of Christ to establish his kingdom on earth. Any hope for society was not to be found in secular government, but through the conversion of adult individuals now and the intervention of Christ in the future.

Although Luther had defined the kingdom of God similarly, he had pointed out that if the lion and lamb lie down together, the lamb needs frequent renewing! While agreeing that a Christian could renounce the sword of the magistrate, Luther believed that a Christian could employ it on behalf of others (Bainton, pp. 153-157).

As the teaching (below) of two eminent Anabaptist leaders demonstrates, the separation of church and state was to be absolute. There was no room for compromise:

> The gospel and its adherents, moreover, are not to be protected by the sword, nor are they thus to protect themselves. . . . True Christian believers are sheep among wolves, sheep for the slaughter. They must be baptized in anguish and affliction, tribulation, persecution, suffering and death. They must be tried with fire, and must reach the Fatherland of eternal rest, not by killing their bodily enemies, but by [mortifying] their [spiritual] enemies. Neither do they use worldly sword or war, since killing has absolutely ceased with them — unless indeed they are under the old law (Conrad Grebel, the chief founder of Swiss Anabaptism, writing in 1524. As quoted by Wenger, p. 17).

It is instructive and challenging to note just how literally sixteenth-century Anabaptists took this teaching. One group of Hutterites, having been granted asylum by Count Leonard of Lichtenstein as they fled from Austrian authorities, felt bound by conscience to leave this haven of refuge when they heard that Count Leonard would meet the Austrians with cannon balls if they attempted to extradite the Anabaptists! They travelled on until they had found a nobleman who would grant them toleration without protection! (Bainton, pp. 156-157).

The strict separation of church and state comes through equally clearly in the writings of Menno Simons:

> The Scriptures teach that there are two opposing princes and two opposing kingdoms: the one is the

Prince of peace; the other the prince of strife. Each of these princes has his particular kingdom and as the prince is, so is his kingdom. The Prince of peace is Christ Jesus; His kingdom is the kingdom of peace, which is His church;His messengers are the messengers of peace; His body is the body of peace; His children are the seed of peace; and His inheritance and reward are the inheritance and reward of peace. In short, with this King, and His kingdom and reign, it is nothing but peace. . . .

O beloved reader, our weapons are not swords and spears, but patience, silence, and hope, and the Word of God. With these we must maintain our heavy warfare and fight our battle. Paul says, the weapons of our warfare are not carnal; but mighty through God. With these we intend to storm the kingdom of the devil; and not with swords, spears, cannon, and coats of mail. For he esteemeth iron as straw, and brass as rotten wood. Thus may we with our Prince, Teacher and Example, Christ Jesus, raise the father against the son, and the son against the father, and may cast down imagination and every high thing that exalteth itself against the knowledge of God, and bring into captivity every thought in obedience to Christ. . . .

The other prince is the prince of darkness, Antichrist, and Satan. This prince is a prince of all tumult and blood. Raging and murder is his proper nature and policy. His commandments and teachings and his kingdom, body, and church are of the same nature (I John 3). . . .

Our opponents invent that we are intent upon rebellion; something of which we have never thought! But we say, and that truthfully, that they and their ancestors for more than a thousand years have been that which they make us out to be. . . .

For what they have done these last few years by their writings, teachings, and cries, cities and countries prove. How neatly they have placed one ruler against others saying, Since the sword is placed in your hands you may maintain the Word of the Lord thereby, until they prevailed on them and have shed human blood like water, torn the hearts from each other's bodies, and have made countless harlots, rogues, widows, and orphans. The innocent citizen they have devoured and plundered; cities and lands they have destroyed. In short, they have done as if neither prophet nor Christ nor apostle nor the Word of God had even been upon the earth. Notwithstanding, they wish to be called the holy, Christian church and body. O dear Lord, how lamentably is Thy holy, worthy Word mocked, and Thy glorious work derided, as if Thy divine and powerful activity in Thy church were nothing but reading, shouting, water, bread, wine, and name; and as if rebellion, warring, robbing, murder, and devilish works were permissible. Dear reader, behold and observe, and learn to know this kingdom and body. For if they with such actions and doings were the body of Christ, as the learned ones assure them, then Christ's holy, glorious kingdom, church, and body would be an inhuman, cruel, rebellious, bloody, rapacious, noisy, unmerciful, and unrighteous people. . . .

The merciful and gracious Lord grant and give you and them wisdom that you may learn to know of what spirit and kingdom you are the children, what you seek, what prince you serve, what doctrine you maintain, what sacraments you have, what fruits you produce, what life you lead, and in what kingdom, body, and church you are incorporated (Menno Simons, 1496-1561, as quoted by Holmes, pp. 185-189).

F. Anabaptists in a Democracy

Many, though not most, Christians today live in democracies. A democratic government to a considerable degree pursues policies which represent the wishes of the majority of the people they govern. In many democracies, a significant proportion of the population claims to be Christian. In such a context, is it not appropriate for Christians, even Anabaptists, to be vitally involved in the political and governing process? This is a question which perplexes a growing number of Anabaptist Christians today. See, for example, the article by Reg Toews, "Can Mennonite Christians Govern?" in the May 2, 1986 issue of *The Messenger*. Here Toews, who is Associate Executive Secretary, Administration and Development, of Mennonite Central Committee, Akron, PA, argues that more Mennonites should enter the civil service ". . . as a Christian calling, by getting involved in school boards, town councils and other levels of government."

There does not seem to be a clear or easy answer to this question. Perhaps the best we can do is acknowledge that the problem is a complex one, and even biblically informed consciences differ in opinion. Christians have always acknowledged that there are certain state directives which a Christian cannot obey, and that sometimes there are state functions in which a Christian cannot participate.

It should come as no surprise to the Christian to discover that his or her agenda seems foolish and naive to the unbeliever. What is disturbing is the widespread agnosticism of professing Christians in the West who, increasingly it seems, have come to equate the Western way of life with Christianity, and who are willing to kill, if need be, to preserve it. Since no nation or way of life endures forever, it is safe to say that not only will the Western way of life vanish, but so also will that form of Christianity which sees as a part of its mandate to defend itself at all costs. Such Christianity makes of God a mere tribal deity.

Perhaps it is time for Christians to redouble their efforts to fulfill their unique mandate. If Christians who do not have the time to get involved in governing are accused of living in a dream world, they need to remind themselves of the true nature of the battle which they must fight, and which they alone are equipped to win. In the words of Origen (A.D. 182-251):

> . . . Celsus urges us "to help the king with all our might, and to labor with him in the maintenance of justice, to fight for him, and if he require it, to fight under him, or lead an army with him." To this our answer is, that we do . . . give help to kings . . . a divine help, "putting on the whole armor of God" (Ephesians 6:11). And this we do in obedience to the injunction of the apostle, "I exhort, therefore, that first of all, supplications, prayers, intercessions, and giving of thanks, be made for all men; for kings, and for all that are in authority" (I Timothy 2:1-2); and the more one excels in piety, the more effective help does he render to kings, even more than is given by soldiers who go forth to fight and slay as many of the enemy as they can. . . . And as we by our prayers vanquish all demons who stir up war, and lead us to the violation of oaths, and disturb the peace, we in this way are much

more helpful to the kings than those who go into the field and fight for them. (See chapter 3 above, "War and the Early Church.")

Let the church *be* and *do* all that God sent Christ into the world to *be* and *do*.

G. Questions for Discussion

1. Should a Christian pay taxes when it is known that these taxes will go to support a war effort?

2. Should a Christian farmer sell grain when he knows that a portion of the grain will go to feed soldiers who are engaged in battle?

3. In *Challenge to the Church: A Theological Comment on the Political Crisis in South Africa* (Published by Theology Global Context, Stony Point Center, Crickettown Road, Stony Point, NY 10983), it is argued that contemporary Christian use of Romans 13:1-7 cannot be justified biblically. Paul, the authors of this booklet argue,

> . . . is simply not addressing the issue of a just or unjust state or the need to change one government for another. He is simply establishing the fact that there will be some kind of secular authority and that Christians as such are not exonerated from subjection to secular laws and authorities. He does not say anything at all about what they should do when the state becomes unjust and oppressive.

The authors conclude that the church must not only take sides unequivocally and consistently with the poor and with victims of injustice, it must also

> . . . actively participate in the struggle for liberation and for a just society. . . . Once it is established that the present regime has no moral legitimacy and is in fact a tyrannical regime, certain things follow for the church. . . . In the first place the church cannot collaborate with tyranny. It cannot or should not do anything that appears to give legitimacy to a morally illegitimate regime. Secondly, the church . . . should mobilize its members. . . to think and work and plan for change of government. . . . And finally, the moral illegitimacy of the . . . regime

means that the church will have to be involved at times
in civil disobedience.

Analyze biblically and be prepared to discuss the point of view
expressed above, using the following questions as a guide:

a. By what criteria is a government's "moral legitimacy" established?

b. What arc some ways the church can "collaborate with tyranny"
(1) actively? (2) passively?

c. If we agree that slavery is a great evil, was Paul's failure to attack
the institution of slavery in his day an example of "collaboration
with tyranny" (See Philemon; Ephesians 6:5-9)?

d. Under what circumstances, and by what means (passive and
active), should the church resist the evil of a state?

H. For Further Reading

Bainton, Roland H. *Christian Attitudes toward War and Peace: A
Historical Survey and Critical Re-evaluation.* Nashville:
Abingdon, 1960 (pp. 152-172).

Hershberger, Guy Franklin. *War, Peace, and Nonresistance.* Scottdale: Herald Press, 1969 (pp. 156-171).

Holmes, Arthur F., ed. *War and Christian Ethics.* Grand Rapids:
Bakcr Book House, 1975 (pp. 137-189).

Wenger, J.C. *Pacifism and Biblical Nonresistance.* Scottdale: Herald
Press, 1968 (pp. 14-26).

Chapter 9
Weakness and Power
in the New Testament

It is frequently argued that pacifism and nonresistance are but thin disguises for cowardice. While this accusation may certainly be justified in some instances, it demonstrates a profound ignorance or oversight of the paradoxical New Testament teaching on weakness and power.

People have always been awed and cowed by power, and our civilization is no exception. Power, whether it be military, intellectual, economic, physical, political or scientific, is worshipped and practised in daily living. We are a privileged people; privileges require protection; protection requires power; the ultimate power is the power to take the life of the one who is seen as a threat to this privilege.

Of course, obedient followers of Christ cannot strive for privilege and power; our task is to practise sharing and self-giving. The church, which is the body of Christ, does not look for a way to wield power, but for ways to serve. This is one part of the message of the cross which, to them that are perishing, is utter foolishness (I Corinthians 1:18-25). On no subject is there a more startling contrast between God's outlook and ours.

A. Jesus

1. **The Incarnation** (Matthew 1:18-25; Luke 1:26-56; 2:1-40; John 1:14).

When Mary was told that her child should be named Jesus because he would liberate his people, it was understandable that she and her contemporaries should have thought of liberation in terms of that which occurred under Moses, or Joshua, or the Maccabean brothers. But of all the millions of souls numbered in the census of Caesar Augustus, the one born in Bethlehem just in time to be counted, must have been, in worldly terms, among the least likely to figure prominently in a world obsessed with brute power.

No news reporters were present, no television cameras were rolling, as the most momentous event in the history of humankind began to unfold with the birth of an illegitimate baby in a barn nearly two thousand years ago. The power of God manifested itself in the weakest of all human creatures, a tiny newborn infant.

Our faith began, not among brilliant minds, not with the wealthy and powerful of that day, not among the exciting, the beautiful or the fascinating; nor did the all-powerful Word begin in the ranks of television personalities, sports heroes or leading journalists of the time. Rather, the Power of God unto salvation began among the peasants, shepherds and an assortment of common barnyard animals.

The audacity of the plan is staggering to the natural mind. The mind that created the universe is now limited to the body of a tiny infant; when hungry, God cannot even ask for food in a dignified manner, but must cry like any other baby, aimlessly moving his tiny limbs and opening and closing minute fists in an effort to communicate human needs to an earthly mother; the one who filled heaven and earth with glory now occupies one or two square feet in the bottom of a manger; the Ruler and Sustainer of the universe must derive sustenance from the breast of a young mother; the All-powerful is now, humanly speaking, powerless, weak and utterly vulnerable.

Christians must never forget that the mortal struggle against "the rulers, against the authorities, against the powers of this dark world and against the spiritual forces of evil in heavenly realms" (Ephesians 6:12) pitted all of the violent power of which Satan was capable against the pathetic weakness of a baby.

2. The Life of Christ

Nor did the strategy of weakness seem to make either sense or headway during the thirty-three years Christ lived on earth. His life is shrouded in obscurity, except for sketchy details of incidents relating to his birth, and a few pages of biographical material relating to the last three years of his life. From this material we know that he spent most of his time in Palestine, an obscure, remote and insignificant part of the vast territories dominated by the Roman Empire. He was a teacher of some note in the eyes of the common people, but a dangerously unorthodox "pain in the neck" to those entrusted with maintaining the purity and the integrity of Jewish faith. There were twelve disciples with whom he engaged in itineration, but none of these was of any significance. He never wrote a book. It seemed impossible to draw him into any discussion of the really big issues of the day, such as the Roman occupation. As a liberator of his people, he obviously had no future at all.

3. The Death of Christ

Jesus died the death of a criminal, apparently unable to answer charges of political insurrection brought against him by the very people whom he, as Messiah, was supposed to liberate. He didn't try to defend either himself or his followers. He seemed impotent and weak, and was easily defeated. His closest followers deserted him in his moment of greatest need. What foolishness! Such refusal to use power was bound to fail! And to all appearances it did fail. Perhaps his mother, as she tearfully observed her precious Son's death agonies, recalled with bitter irony the joyful outpouring of hopes and expectations with which she had greeted the news that her child would liberate Israel (Luke 1:46-55). How naive she had been then! How differently things had turned out for her Son: he had not brought down rulers from their thrones, they had brought him down; he had tried to lift up the humble, but had been trampled by them in return; he had on occasion filled the hungry with good things, and sent the rich away empty, but the rich were having their revenge now. Power had overcome weakness once again.

B. Paul

1. The Persecutor

As a Pharisee, Saul (Paul) was concerned that the Law of God be carried out in its entirety. He took God seriously and therefore he took the law seriously. He was concerned with the purity of the Jewish faith, understanding that to be the path to national blessing and restoration. In persecuting members of the Jewish sect, who followed the teachings of Christ and who would eventually come to be called "Christians," Saul was trying to achieve the admirable goal of maintaining the orthodoxy of Judaism. The Old Testament was filled with precedents for the action which he took against the early Christians. Moses, Joshua, Samuel, David, Elijah, Ezra, Nehemiah and many others had employed violence in an attempt to ensure the victory of good over evil. Saul's use of violent power was understandable and justifiable (Acts 7:54-60; 8:1-3; 9:1-3; 22:1-5). To resort to mortal violence in order to protect and preserve from destruction that which is cherished is the basis of all justified violence.

2. The Persecuted

With his conversion on the Damascus road came a transformation in Paul's view of weakness and power. He recognized not only
that the security which is sought through power and expressed in
violence is an illusion but also that the power of the gospel is
diametrically opposite. God's great power was demonstrated, not
in the brutal subjugation of dangerous enemies, but in Christ's
submission to death on the cross at the hands of his enemies. Not
the crucifier, but the Crucified, helps us to make sense out of life.

Having understood this, Paul lived out his life accordingly, frequently writing about the power of weakness, frequently himself
being the object of violence, and finally suffering execution under
Nero, "weak" victim of a "powerful" and violent emperor. Paul's
writings are sprinkled with statements attesting to his radical views
on weakness and power and to his faithfulness to the crucified
Christ:

> God chose the weak things of the world to shame the
> strong (I Corinthians 1:27).
> I came to you in weakness and fear, and with much
> trembling (I Corinthians 2:3).
> For it seems to me that God has put us apostles on
> display at the end of the procession, like men con-
> demned to die in the arena. We have been made a
> spectacle to the whole universe, to angels as well as to
> men. We are fools for Christ, but you are so wise in
> Christ! We are weak but you are strong! You are
> honored, we are dishonored! To this very hour we go
> hungry and thirsty, we are in rags, we are brutally
> treated, we are homeless. We work hard with our own
> hands. When we are cursed, we bless; when we are
> persecuted, we endure it; when we are slandered, we
> answer kindly. Up to this moment we have become the
> scum of the earth, the refuse of the world. . . . I urge you
> to imitate me (I Corinthians 4:9-13,16).
> But we have this treasure in jars of clay to show that
> this all-surpassing power is from God and not from us.
> We are hard pressed on every side, but not crushed;
> perplexed, but not in despair; persecuted, but not
> abandoned; struck down, but not destroyed. We always
> carry around in our body the death of Jesus, so that the

life of Jesus may also be revealed in our body. For we who are alive are always being given over to death for Jesus' sake, so that his life may be revealed in our mortal body (II Corinthians 4:7-11).

If I must boast, I will boast of the things that show my weakness (II Corinthians 11:30).

To keep me from becoming conceited . . . there was given me a thorn in my flesh, a messenger of Satan, to torment me. Three times I pleaded with the Lord to take it away from me. But he said to me, "My grace is sufficient for you, for my power is made perfect in weakness." Therefore I will boast all the more gladly about my weaknesses, so that Christ's power may rest on me. That is why, for Christ's sake, I delight in weaknesses, in insults, in hardships, in persecutions, in difficulties. For when I am weak, then I am strong (II Corinthians 12:7-10).

It is clear that the natural world cannot understand or accept this view of weakness and power. It is the way of the cross. The cross looks like defeat, but in fact means victory.

C. The Contemporary Church

Any Christian contemplating a personal role in his or her nation's wars should reflect carefully on a number of questions: (1) Should a Christian take an active part in the lethal violence advocated by the state? (2) Can a Christian's participation in the general killing of war be a glorification of the name of Jesus Christ? (3) Can it be a positive witness to our Saviour's self-giving love? (4) Can it be an evident and indisputable expression of a Christian's imitation of and loyal obedience to Jesus? (5) Can it be an incarnate, living testimony of the Son of God crucified and resurrected so that all persons might have life? (6) Can it be an evidence of the fruit of God's Spirit within us?

I believe the answer to these questions must be "No." But Christians have always been tempted to construct a theology of glory which dispenses with the cross (I Corinthians 2:2); to fight violence with violence; to meet power with power.

For thousands of years, people have sought security through violence. It has never worked for more than short periods of time. The evolution of weapons, from clubs to longbows, from chariots to tanks, from slings to nuclear missiles, each calculated to deter aggressive neighbours, demonstrates the impotence of worldly power in curbing violence.

Violence breeds hatred, resentment, and more violence, never peace or love. The law of the harvest applies in the realm of violence as elsewhere: we reap what we sow (Galatians 6:7); grapes are not gathered from thorns (Matthew 7:16). The cross is the only way of victory over the power of evil.

The way of the cross is not for cowards. But Jesus called "weak" men and women to follow this path in fighting evil (Matthew 10:16,38; 16:24-25; Luke 9:23,24; Mark 10:39-45; John 10:15-16). In the words of Lasserre, "In the cross, where Christ's life found its most complete expression, lies the secret of all Christian action" (p. 68).

D. Conclusion

We walk by faith. Faith sees and interprets the present in the context of not only the past, but the future. Faith takes the long view, not the short view. Viewed in this way, it is evident that those things accomplished by violence in the past have not endured. Where, today, are the world's once mightiest nations: Egypt? Babylon? Persia? Greece? Rome? Britain? The poet Shelley has aptly described the transience and long-term futility of those who rely upon violence to maintain their privilege:

> I met a traveler from an antique land
> Who said: "Two vast and trunkless legs of stone
> Stand in the desert. Near them, on the sand,
> Half sunk, a shattered visage lies, whose frown,
> And wrinkled lip, and sneer of cold command,
> Tell that its sculptor well those passions read
> Which yet survive, stamped on these lifeless things,
> The hand that mocked them and the heart that fed.
> And on the pedestal, these words appear:
>   'My name is Ozymandias, king of kings:
>   Look on my works, ye Mighty, and despair.'
> Nothing beside remains. Round the decay
> Of that colossal wreck, boundless and bare,
> The lone and level sands stretch far away."
> ("Ozymandias" by Percy Bysshe Shelley, 1792-1822)

On the other hand, the existence of nearly 1.6 billion professing Christians today, many of them living and spiritually flourishing in

78

the most hostile and violently repressive environments, proves the vitality of God's strength made perfect in weakness. The cross may look foolish and even crazy, but only that which is accomplished through the cross has the power to endure.

As Yoder puts it:

> The Cross is what makes history move, even if we've been told the opposite in our national mythology, according to which world leadership is measured in megatonnage, and in our media morality dramas, where every plot problem is resolved by a gun, and in our local economic dramas, where every employment problem is resolved by a federal weapons contract (*He Came Preaching Peace*. Scottdale: Herald Press, 1985. p. 46).

Edith Schaeffer, in an essay entitled "Unequal Equipment" (appearing in *Christianity Today,* October 11, 1974, pp. 33-34), contrasts the power persons deploy with the weakness used by God to win victories. "It is not only interesting but very important to consider how God has equipped the people to whom he has given especially hard tasks at crisis moments of history," she comments. Among those whom God has so equipped, she cites Paul, David, Gideon, and Elijah as examples. She concludes that " . . . there is a purpose in the inequality of the equipment. . . . [It] serves to demonstrate God's existence and power and glory" rather than people's.

E. Questions for Discussion

1. Read Matthew 5:23-24, 43-48; 6:12-15; 18:21-35; Mark 11:25; Ephesians 4:32; Colossians 3:13.

2. In what sense may it be said that failure to forgive is an essential element in all lethal violence? Is it possible to simultaneously kill and forgive one's enemies?

3. Are there situations in which God does not require the Christian to forgive? If so, list and discuss some of these, supporting your answer with Scripture. If not, discuss the problem of a Christian's forgiveness of his or her nation's mortal enemies.

4. Should Christians practise a dual ethic, one for private life and one for public life?

5. Discuss some of the possible social and personal implications of forgiveness in a time of war.

6. In what sense and by whose standards are those who practise

forgiveness stronger than those who refuse to forgive?

7. What are likely to be some of the negative/positive consequences of forgiveness as a lifestyle?

8. In what sense is faith the key to forgiveness of one's enemies?

9. How can we grow in faith?

F. For Further Reading

Donnelly, Doris. *Putting Forgiveness into Practice.* Allen, Texas: Argus Communications, 1982.

Kooiman, Helen. *Forgiveness in Action.* New York: Hawthorn Books, 1974.

Lasserre, Jean. *War and the Gospel.* London: James Clarke & Co., 1962.

Sanders, J. Oswald. *Paul the Leader.* Eastbourne: Kingsway, 1983.

Sider, Ronald J. "The Way of the Cross in the Nuclear Age," in *Perspectives on Peacemaking,* edited by John Bernbaum. Glendale: Regal Books, 1984.

Yoder, John H. *He Came Preaching Peace.* Scottdale: Herald Press, 1985.

Appendix

Mennonite Statements on Peace

The cooperating publishers of this book each have an official position on the issue of peace in their constitutions and/or statements of faith. They vary in their formulations and are exerpted below.

Chortizer Mennonite Conference: Constitution
Article 10, a.
Nonresistance

The Christian shall live peaceably with all men, not take revenge or be offensive, but show mercy and love taught and exemplified by Jesus Christ, the Prince of Peace. The teaching of Jesus not to resist evil means that every Christian shall renounce all violence in human relations. Love is to be shown to all men. This applies to every area of life: to personal injustice, to situations in which people commonly resort to litigation, to industrial strife, and to international tensions and wars. As non-resistant Christians, we cannot support war in any way as an officer, soldier, or by giving direct financial support, whether combatant or non-combatant. It shall be the obligation of the spiritual members of the church to deal redemptively with members erring in nonresistance. We must even at the risk of life, aggressively do whatever we can to alleviate human distress and suffering. We are ministers of reconciliation and peacemakers (Matthew 5:38, 39; Romans 12:17-21; Hebrews 12:14; John 18:35; I Corinthians 6:1ff; II Corinthians 6:14).

Conference of Mennonites in Canada: Constitution and Bylaws (1986)
Excerpt from General Bylaws, Section II.

We believe that Christ lived and taught the way of life as recorded in the Scriptures, which is God's plan for individuals and all humankind; and that it becomes disciples of Christ to live in this way, thus manifesting in their personal and social life and relationships the love and holiness of God. And we believe that his way of life also implies nonresistance to evil by carnal means, the fullest exercise of love, and the resolute abandonment of the use of violence including warfare. We believe further that the Christian life will of necessity express itself in nonconformity to the world in life and conduct.

Evangelical Mennonite Conference: Constitution and Bylaws (1981)
Statement of Faith, Article XI
Of Discipleship and Non-Conformity

We believe that there are two opposing kingdoms to which men give their spiritual allegiance, that of Christ and that of Satan. Those who belong to Satan's kingdom live for sin and self, and refuse the obedience of faith (Eph. 2:1-10).

Those who belong to the kingdom of Christ seek:

1. To live holy lives and regard their bodies as temples of the Holy Spirit and crucify their flesh with its affections and lusts (Titus 2:11-14; II Thess. 3:6; Rom. 13:14).

2. To avoid any unequal yoke with unbelievers (II Cor. 6: 14-18; Rom. 12: 1, 2; Eph. 5:11).

3. To walk in love towards God and man refraining from carnal strife and contentions in all areas of life, from war (Rom. 12:14-21) and from swearing oaths (Matt. 5:33-37; James 5:12); to exercise proper stewardship of time, possessions and abilities (I Cor. 16:1,2; II Cor. 8 and 9). Their daily Christian walk should manifest complete allegiance to Christ (I John 2:15-17; II Thess. 3:6; I Peter 2:9).

Church Practices, Article 12
Nonresistance

The Christian shall live peaceably with all men, not take revenge or be offensive, but show mercy and love as taught and exemplified by Jesus Christ, the Prince of Peace. The teaching of Jesus not to resist evil means that every Christian shall renounce all violence in human relations. Love is to be shown to all men. This applies to every area of life: to personal injustice, to situations in which people commonly resort to litigation, to industrial strife, and to international tensions and wars. As nonresistant Christians, we cannot support war in any way as an officer, soldier, or by giving direct financial support, whether combatant or non-combatant. It shall be the obligation of the spiritual members of the church to deal redemptively with members erring in nonresistance. We must even, at the risk of life, aggressively do whatever we can to alleviate human distress and suffering. We are ministers of reconciliation and peacemakers (Matt. 5:38, 39; Rom. 12:17-21; Heb. 12:14; John 18:35; I Cor. 5: 1ff; II Cor. 6:14).

82

Evangelical Mennonite Mission Conference: Constitution (1973)
The Confession of Faith, Article II, Section 8
Discipleship
We believe that Jesus Christ not only taught the way of life by practical example, He walked in it, and that it is God's plan that every individual, as well as all mankind, should walk this way. Further we believe that it is imperative for every follower of Christ to reveal the love and holiness of God through their personal as well as social life. This includes:
1. We believe in the biblical teaching of nonresistance (Matt. 5:38-47, 7:12, 20:25-27; Acts 5:29). 2. We believe in non-swearing of the oath (Matt. 5:34-37; James 5:12). 3. We believe in non-conformity to the world (II Cor. 6:14-18; Rom. 12:1-2). 4. We believe in living a simple life (II Cor. 1:12).

General Conference of Mennonite Brethren Churches: Confession of Faith (1976)
Article XV
Love and Nonresistance
We believe that Christians should live by the law of love and practice the forgiveness of enemies as taught and exemplified by the Lord Jesus. The church, as the body of Christ, is a fellowship of redeemed, separated people, controlled by redemptive love. Its evangelistic responsibility is to present Christ, the Prince of Peace, as the answer to human need, enmity and violence. The evil, brutal and inhuman nature of war stands in contradiction to the new nature of the Christian. The Christian seeks to practice Christ's law of love in all relationships, and in all situations, including those involving personal injustice, social upheaval and international tensions. We believe that it is not God's will that Christians take up arms in military service but that where possible, they perform alternate service to reduce strife, alleviate suffering and bear witness to the love of Christ (Ex.20:1-17; Mt. 5:17-28, 38-45; Rom. 12:19-21; 13:8-10; I Pet.2:19-23).

For Further Reading
(highly recommended sources are marked
by an asterisk *)

A. Books and Pamphlets

Arnold, Eberhard. *The Early Christians After the Death of the Apostles.* Translated from the German by John S. Hoyland, Etta Wilms, and Kathleen E. Hasenberg. Ashton Keynes, Wilts: The Plough Publishing House, 1939.

* Bainton, Roland. *Christian Attitudes toward War and Peace.* Nashville: Abingdon Press, 1960.

Beachey, Duane. *Faith in a Nuclear Age: A Christian Response to War.* Scottdale: Herald Press, 1983.

Bernbaum, John A., ed. *Perspectives on Peacemaking: Biblical Options in the Nuclear Age.* Glendale: Regal Books, 1984.

Clouse, Robert, ed. *War: Four Christian Views.* Downers Grove: InterVarsity Press, 1981.

* Cullmann, Oscar. *The State in the New Testament.* New York: Charles Scribner's Sons, 1956.

Culver, Robert Duncan. *The Peacemongers: A Biblical Answer to Pacifism and Nuclear Disarmament.* Wheaton: Tyndale House, 1985.

Durland, William R. *No King But Caesar? A Catholic Lawyer Looks at Christian Violence.* Scottdale: Herald Press, 1975.

Eller, Vernard. *Christian Anarchy: Jesus' Primacy over the Powers.* Grand Rapids: Eerdmans, 1987.

Ellul, Jacques. *Violence: Reflections from a Christian Perspective.* New York: Seabury, 1969.

Geisler, Norman L. *Ethics: Alternatives and Issues.* Grand Rapids: Zondervan, 1971.

* Helgeland, John, Robert J. Daly and J. Patout Burns. *Christians and the Military: The Early Experience.* Philadelphia: Fortress Press, 1985.

* Hershberger, Guy. *War, Peace, and Nonresistance.* Scottdale: Herald Press, 1969.

Holmes, Arthur F., ed. *War and Christian Ethics.* Grand Rapids: Baker, 1975.

84

* Hornus, Jean-Michel. *It is not Lawful for Me to Fight: Early Christian Attitudes toward War, Violence, and the State.* Revised edition. Scottdale: Herald Press, 1980.

* Lasserre, Jean. *War and the Gospel.* London: James Clarke & Co., 1962.

Lind, Millard C. *Yahweh is a Warrior: The Theology of Warfare in Ancient Israel.* Scottdale: Herald Press, 1980.

* McSorley, Richard. *New Testament Basis of Peacemaking.* Scottdale: Herald Press, 1985.

Morrison, Clinton. *The Mission of the Church and Civil Government.* A Church Peace Mission Pamphlet. Washington, D.C.: The Church Peace Mission, 1964.

Penner, Archie. *A Christian Conscience and Politics.* Steinbach: EMC, 1959.

Sider, Ronald J. *Christ and Violence.* Scottdale: Herald Press, 1979.

* Steiner, Susan Clemmer. *Joining the Army that Sheds no Blood.* Scottdale: Herald Press, 1982.

* Swartley, Willard. *Slavery, Sabbath, War and Women: Case Issues in Biblical Interpretation.* Scottdale: Herald Press, 1983.

Verduin, Leonard. *The Anatomy of a Hybrid: A Study in Church-State Relationships.* Grand Rapids: Eerdmans, 1976.

Wenger, J.C. *Pacifism and Biblical Nonresistance.* Scottdale: Herald Press, 1968.

Wood James E., Jr. *The Problem of Nationalism in Church-State Relationships.* Focal Pamphlet No. 18. Scottdale: Herald Press, 1968.

* Yoder, John Howard. *The Christian Witness to the State.* Institute of Mennonite Studies Series; Number 3. Newton: Faith and Life Press, 1964.

----------. *He Came Preaching Peace.* Scottdale: Herald Press, 1985.

----------. *Nevertheless: The Varieties and Shortcomings of Religious Pacifism.* Scottdale: Herald Press, 1971.

----------. *The Politics of Jesus.* Grand Rapids: Eerdmans, 1972.

----------. *Reinhold Niebuhr and Christian Pacifism.* A Church Peace Mission Pamphlet. Scottdale: Herald Press, 1968.

----------. *What Would You Do? A Serious Answer to a Standard Question.* Scottdale: Herald Press, 1983.

----------. *When War Is Unjust: Being Honest in Just-War Thinking.* Minneapolis: Augsburg, 1984.

Zorn, Raymond 0. *Church and Kingdom.* Philadelphia: Presbyterian and Reformed Publishing Co., 1962.

B. Articles

Bennett, John C. "A Christian View of the State." *Journal of Religious Thought*, 8, no. 2 (1951).

Bray, Gerald. "The Origins of the Christian State." *Churchman*, 99, no. 1 (1985).

Cranfield, C.E.B. "Politics and Christianity." *His* (October 1964).

Dawson, Joseph M. "The Christian View of the State." *Christianity Today*, 1 (July 24, 1957).

* Eller, Vernard. "Romans 13 (actually Romans 12:14-13:8) Re-examined." *TSF Bulletin*, 10 (January-February 1987).

* Fastiggi, Robert and Wayne Teasdale. "Christianity and Politics: Historical Overview and the Contemporary Challenge." *Journal of Dharma: An International Quarterly of World Religions*, 7 (January — March 1982).

* Frend W.H.C. "Prelude to the Great Persecution: The Propaganda War." *Journal of Ecclesiastical History*, 38, no. 1 (January 1987).

Garrett, James L. "The Dialectic of Romans 13:1-7 and Revelation 13: Part One." *Journal of Church and State*, 18 (Autumn 1976).

----------. "The Dialectic of Romans 13:1-7 and Revelation 13: Part Two." *Journal of Church and State*, 19 (Winter 1977).

Klaassen, Walter. "The Anabaptist Understanding of the Separation of the Church." *Church History*, 46 (December 1977).

Mackay, John A. "Religion and Government: Their Separate Spheres and Reciprocal Responsibilities." *Theology Today*, 9 (July 1951)

* O'Donovan, Oliver. "The Political Thought of the Book of Revelation." *Tyndale Bulletin*, 37 (1986).

Peterson, Walfred. "The Christian Attitude Toward the State." *His*, 17 (December 1956).

Scott, Ernest Findlay. "Citizens of Two Worlds: The Individual Christian and the State," *Interpretation*, 4 (October 1950).

Stagg, Frank. "Rendering to Caesar What Belongs to Caesar: Christian Engagement with the World," *Journal of Church and State*, 18 (Winter 1976).

Vonck, Pol. "All Authority Comes from God: Romans 13:1-7 — a Tricky Text about Obedience to Political Power." *After: African Ecclesiastical Review*, 26 (December 1984).

Weber, Hans-Ruedi. "Power: Some Biblical Perspectives." *The Ecumenical Review*, 38, no. 3 (July 1986).

—